**THE ULTIMATE IN GRAPHIC DESIGNER'S AND ILLUSTRATOR'S SELF-PROMOTION**

# PROMO 1

# THE ULTIMATE IN GRAPHIC DESIGNER'S AND ILLUSTRATOR'S SELF-PROMOTION

# PROMO 1

ROSE DeNEVE

CINCINNATI, OHIO

# PROMO 1

Copyright 1990 by North Light Books

94 93 92 91 90    5 4 3 2 1

**Library of Congress Cataloging in Publication Data**

Promo 1 / [compiled by] Rose DeNeve.
     p.   cm.
     ISBN 0-89134-344-X
     1. Commercial art—Marketing.    I. DeNeve, Rose.
  NC1001.6.P7   1990
   741.6'068'8—dc20                90-30723
                                  CIP

Edited by Kathleen Friel and Susan Conner

Designed by Cathleen Norz

The permissions starting on page 156 constitute an extension of this copyright page.

# ACKNOWLEDGMENTS

I would like to thank David Lewis at North Light Books for suggesting I take on the job. Also at North Light, thanks are due to Kathleen Friel, who smoothed development stages of the project, and Susan Conner, who took over its day-to-day management.

Like any large-scale endeavor, compiling this book became the subject of many conversations and requests for assistance. Along these lines, particular thanks are due to Martin Fox and Carol Stevens, of *Print* magazine, and Margaret Richarson, formerly of *HOW* magazine, for their suggestions and invaluable assistance in locating possible contributors.

But the real stars of this project are all the designers and illustrators who lent their work for inclusion and who shared with me their thoughts about promoting the business of visual communication. Many of them went to some trouble to find additional materials and prepare photography and artwork especially for this volume. To these professionals whose work appears in this book, a heartfelt thanks.

# CONTENTS

# INTRODUCTION

In the past decade, a remarkable phenomenon transpired: The business of graphic design and illustration—at one time known widely as "commercial art"—came of age. In the process, the perception of those who create graphic art shifted dramatically, from paste-up-person-cum-decorator to visual communication specialist. Graphic design firms were no longer studios or ateliers but profit centers to be acquired by multi-national agencies. Young designers and illustrators began entering the field in unprecedented numbers, each hoping for a piece of the enticing but, alas, somewhat limited pie.

As graphic arts—and by this term, we mean all of the varied skills that go into printed communications—became a more competitive business, they also became more marketable and eminently promotable.

In today's business climate, few graphic artists would deny the need to market and promote their services. Even those who have never produced a self-promotion piece see the need for one and, given the right mix of time and money, would probably create one. Those who do promote their talents find several advantages.

First, there is the obvious gain in visibility among the artist's market of choice. As one graphic designer put it, a promotion predisposes a buyer to consider you for a job. You can't win a race you haven't entered.

But given the competition, how do you produce a promotion piece that is truly successful? Are complicated marketing strategies really necessary? And how do you measure a promotion's success anyway?

The 72 promotions and campaigns represented in *PROMO 1: The Ultimate in Graphic Designer's and Illustrator's Self-Promotion* can't really provide any fail-safe answers. Rather, they offer insight into particular needs and processes and suggest how well a particular self-promotion met those needs.

Sometimes a promotion's success is self-evident—the phone starts ringing as soon as it hits the street. But more often, the effect of self-promotion is difficult to quantify and likely builds over time. This doesn't mean that all self-promotion should be conceived in terms of a coordinated campaign of multiple, related pieces sent methodically throughout the year. But it does mean that effective promotion will be created within a stratagem—that is, through *thinking*—as a definitive statement within a larger marketing effort; as a series of mailers, each touting another area of the artist's expertise; as a memorable holiday greeting; or as a clever moving announcement. An effective promotion can be as simple as an elegant poster or as complicated as a graphic identity system and comprehensive marketing plan.

If the projects presented here reveal anything clearly, it is that there is no one "right" way to promote oneself or one's business in the graphic arts. There are as many effective approaches as there are designers and illustrators, and as many solutions as there are needs. Each artist faces his own set of parameters and works within his own style.

Still, some generalities can be drawn. The first (and perhaps most obvious) one is that a younger designer/illustrator or newer business configuration will likely need more—and more dynamic—promotion pieces than a more established artist or concern. Just as consumer product companies mount an aggressive new product launch, so graphic artists must approach their own entries into the graphic design marketplace. Similarly, as a design or illustration business grows and matures, promotions may be needed to call attention to new skills or widening capabilities. Indeed, an entire business and its market may need to be redefined for its potential customers.

A second generality to be drawn is that a successful self-promotion, like any successful visual communication, will exhibit a certain sense of *appropriateness* both to its audience and its message. A corporate designer, for example, might show off annual report projects in a crisply styled and lavishly printed capabilities brochure, but send a glittery plastic ornament as a Christmas greeting, with no apparent inconsistency.

Nor, from the evidence here, does an effective self-promotion have to cost a lot. Many of the examples in this book were produced at less than one dollar per copy; others were produced at cost or in trade with printers, separation houses, photographers, typographers, and/or others in the business.

And, be they lavish or restrained, the most effective self-promotions are *clearly conceived,* from a *unique point of view.* They celebrate the *individuality* of the artist or designer and reflect his or her own working style, convincing the buyer by speaking the buyer's language. That may mean stretching the envelope a bit, pushing creativity beyond what a client would normally buy, to reveal what's possible with the right effort.

The best promotions also have a good deal of *entertainment value.* Wit, humor, cleverness, unusual production techniques, unexpected copy, spectacular or intriguing imagery—all help get the message read.

And good promotions are *useful.* From the loud sales pitch to the low-key studio/artist signature, an effective promotion tells a prospect why to hire you as well as how. It provides interesting and valuable information by concept (a calendar/mailer), context (a holiday greeting), or content (a capabilities piece).

All of the above, conscientiously applied, yield a self-promotion with *staying power.* In the words of one successful graphic designer, "Effective promotion isn't thrown away. If it is, that promotion isn't working as hard as it should."

So. Follow the rules and your own self-promotion will land bigger and better-paying jobs with unlimited creative potential, right?

Not necessarily. Anyone who thinks their business success relies solely on promotion isn't thinking very far ahead. There are many other factors entering into it: the artist's or designer's reliability, cooperativeness, productivity, inventiveness, ability to communicate both verbally and visually, artistic style and temperament, and sheer talent all play a role, as do the local, regional, and national economies and the vaguries of fashion.

But a carefully planned self-promotion gets you noticed. It introduces you to prospects, familiarizes them with your work, gets your foot in the door. It can even straightaway land an assignment.

**But the rest—the *real* success—is up to you.**

—Rose DeNeve

## LETTER PERFECT

*Paul Shaw/*
*Letter Design*
*New York, New York*

By leaving out the flash and dazzle, Paul Shaw's simply designed promotions focus the recipient's attention on the artist's not inconsiderable skills in calligraphy. At the core of this scheme is an "Alphabet" series, a yearly effort that costs three to five hundred dollars each time and keeps the artist's name— and talents— before the eyes of current and potential clients. (Some of the alphabets have been framed and hung on clients' walls.) The alphabets are augmented by occasional other pieces—a postcard showing hand-lettered typefaces, for example, or a moving announcement. As simple as they are, these mailers have been more than modestly successful—one, produced for the cost of mailing alone, garnered several letter-design jobs; another brought Shaw continuing work with a Soho gallery as a full-service designer.

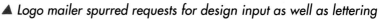

▲ *Logo mailer spurred requests for design input as well as lettering*

▲ *A more ambitious project, Letterforms serves as a calligraphy textbook as well as*
*a style reference for clients. Copies are also sold through independent booksellers*

▲ Shaw's "Alphabet" mailer

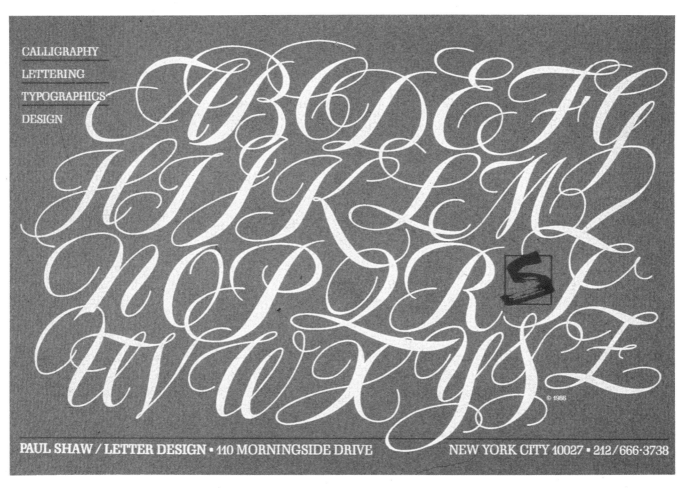

CALLIGRAPHY
LETTERING
TYPOGRAPHICS
DESIGN

PAUL SHAW / LETTER DESIGN • 110 MORNINGSIDE DRIVE     NEW YORK CITY 10027 • 212/666-3738

▲ Postcard worked with Spencerian alphabet to increase commissions for
handdrawn letterforms—most notably for the movie and television industries

## CONCERTED EFFORTS

*Pentagram Design
London, England;
New York, New York; and
San Francisco, California*

Pentagram Design is a unique design partnership. Founded in London in 1962 by some of that country's leading design thinkers and practitioners, the firm has since added partners in New York and San Francisco. Each of these partners has brought style, skills, and strength to what the partnership itself calls a "constituted federal system"; the partnership known as Pentagram, by this token, becomes the facilitating agent for those styles and skills. Pentagram promotion is a facet of facilitation. Yet it is more. Elegant, tasteful, thoughtful, inventive, warm—these attributes work to create an image of the partnership as more cultured, more considerate, than other design firms. That this image has been well established can be judged by the amount of positive publicity the firm and its promotions receive, and by the reputation for excellence it enjoys among clients, colleagues, design students and historians, design journalists, and all those associated by work or interest with the field of graphic design.

▲ Living by Design, *the first book about Pentagram's work and ideas, was published in an intimate softcover volume in 1978*

▲ Ideas on Design, *the hardcover sequel to* Living by Design, *published in 1986*

PROMOTION
When promotion just meant advertising, promotional design was largely the province of the advertising agencies. But more sophisticated and broader marketing concepts increasingly demand more dedicated design skills. Posters and presentations, books and brochures–these often have to account for both corporate identity and brand image while creating their own distinct impact. Pentagram takes on this work sometimes on an individual project basis, sometimes as a continuing service at a consultancy level. It provides scope for wit and style, as well as the opportunity to uncover new aspects of the organization represented and to communicate them with creativity and originality.
LogoParis
July
June
AMERICAN PRESIDENT LINES

*A collection of recent projects, the Pentagram "Review" documents the firm's range of capabilities and fills the need to explain the partnership to prospective clients*

▲ *Selections from Pentagram Papers, which "publish examples of curious, entertaining, stimulating, provocative and occasionally controversial points of view that have come to the attention of, or in some cases are actually originated by, Pentagram"*

▲ *No. 14, on partner Kit Hinrichs's collection of American flags and flag artifacts*

▲ *"Pasta Pentagrama" included recipes from the chefs in the London and New York offices*

## A MARKETABLE IMAGE

*Wallace Church*
*Associates*
*New York, New York*

As imagery consultants to top U.S. consumer products corporations, Wallace Church Associates create visual personalities for both packaged goods and their manufacturers. When it came to devising a visual identity for their own business, therefore, principals Stanley Church and Bob Wallace wanted a system of promotional materials that would suggest both its design-driven philosophy and its strong marketing expertise. The most critical element in the system is a new "brochure"—actually, a number of loose sheets encased in a glossy black folder. At a cost of ten dollars per copy, these books are used selectively and strategically; pages can be added or rearranged to highlight particular projects. And the investment has paid off handsomely: the new brochure was key in landing more than three dozen new, major packaging assignments in its first year alone. Other, even whimsical pieces—including greetings and announcements—are designed within the same elegant parameters and together create a distinctive impression for the firm.

▲ *Wallace Church's seasonal greetings may take different forms but are always packaged with the right image. Moreover, the designers report that at least half of the "Christmas Loupes" are still in use by clients*

▲ *Elegant packaging for an invitation to an office opening party clearly communicates "fun" inside*

▲ Wallace Church's self-promotion brochure

## CHAMPION OF PROMOTION

*James Miho*
*Pasadena, California*

Designer James Miho's association with papermaker Champion International has been long and fruitful. With his client's dedication to helping designers best use their products, Miho enjoys a wide latitude in developing paper- and printing-oriented promotions. Always handsome, these have ranged from posters and folders to complex brochures and three-dimensional packages. But among the lushest are those produced to boost sales of Champion's top-end cast-coated products, Kromekote, Kromekote 2000, and Colorcast. Because these papers are profitable, and because designers and printers are sometimes apprehensive about using them, Miho's work here has been first instructional—how to get best results on a cast-coated paper—and at the same time delightful, earning him an enviable reputation among his peers.

▲ *Produced at twenty thousand dollars for thirty thousand copies, Miho's intimately scaled (four-inch square) "China" is a diary of his own travels in that Eastern land; in addition to reinforcing Champion's international stance, it noticeably increased Kromekote sales*

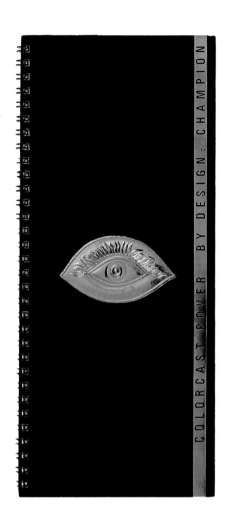

▲ A full-range production promotion for Colorcast Cover features foil stamping, die-cuts, press tips, and interesting tidbits from the history of design

## STRATEGIES FOR SUCCESS

*Landor Associates
San Francisco,
California*

The client roster at Landor Associates, a San Francisco-based design and image consultancy, reads like a *Who's Who* of international corporations. According to the *Economist*, Landor is the largest such firm in the United States—in the world, says the *Financial Times*. To speak to its top-notch clientele, Landor has devised a system of promotional materials that is as handsome as it is practical. Tied together by Landor's own black-and-red corporate color scheme, the system ranges from a 166-page, full-color, perfect-bound book to folios about the company or individual projects, a quarterly newsletter, a reprint system, and a T-shirt. Each also bears the company's official stamp of sorts—a line engraving of the ferryboat *Klamath*, Landor's world headquarters, moored in San Francisco Bay. While developing such a comprehensive system was a major undertaking, its visual cohesiveness and premier production not only shows what Landor sells; it's also a strategic element in keeping Landor Associates where they are—on top.

▲ Landor Associates' promotional materials system

▲ A concise overview of Landor clients and capabilities,

the "Mini-Brochure" is used in tandem with folios about individual projects

▲ *The centerpiece—a compendium of strategic design projects for clients the world over—is left behind with key corporate officers after a sales call*

▲ *Image Matters, Landor's design-oriented quarterly newsletter, reports internally to the company's six international offices and externally to clients and friends*

## TO THE POINT

*Carbone Smolan*
*Associates*
*New York, New York*

Like the projects they produce for their corporate and institutional clients, the promotions by Carbone Smolan Associates are directed toward specific marketing goals. Their own capabilities book, entitled *Ten*, expounds on just that aspect of the design firm's philosophy: Each client has a unique communications problem, so each deserves a unique and creative solution. Showing firsthand the quality of Carbone Smolan's work, this book has repaid its thirty-five thousand dollar price tag many times over by successfully bringing in new business. On a smaller scale, a colorful fold-out aims at generating excitement for a dessert cookbook designed by the firm; this piece received great verbal response and also generated a significant number of orders of the book. Finally, a promotion for Paper Sources International, explaining the range and versatility of its Conqueror Cover Bristol sheet, has also met with positive response.

▲ *Fold-out promotes cookbook design by Carbone Smolan; opened size is 6¹/₄ x 28*

▲ *Paper promotion for Paper Sources International*

▲ Capabilities book for Carbone Smolan Associates addresses unique aspects of clients' communications problems

## THE HARD AND THE SOFT

*Ken White + Associates*
*Los Angeles, California*

Promotion from graphic designers Ken White + Associates takes two tacks—a hard-selling, corporate-oriented, case history folder and a series of softer pieces designed to balance it. Each promotion piece, according to Ken White, has a strategy all its own, and while the corporate "kit" sets out to rationally convince prospective clients that the firm can solve their design problems, the other category of promotion works on multiple levels. "These represent fun things that interest us," White explains. "They show our creative side and that we're not afraid of poking fun at ourselves." A case in point is a Christmas greeting that has White himself strung up in lights. In a more serious, if esoteric, vein, a brochure called "White on White" features works on that theme by photographer and illustrator colleagues. Pieces like this, White feels, bring a deeply felt emotional response that is far more captivating than a purely intellectual involvement. At only fifty cents per copy, the "White on White" book was particularly successful, in that it not only generated phone calls and major design awards but also brought in several new clients.

▲ *An invitation to a new office celebration also points up White + Associates'*
*longevity and success. Clever copy hits appropriate color splashes at the right*
*time: "Way back in 1968 when White was green, he helped blue clients see*
*black. Today, White is as good as gold and in his sunny new offices continues*
*to create design that has White's clients and friends tickled pink"*

▲ Christmas greetings reveal a more creative, less formal side of Ken White + Associates. The white-tailed deer and other white-touched animals received their red noses by hand

▲ When Swimmer Cole Martinez Curtis and MTH Design Group shortened their name to Cole Martinez Curtis, they felt they were too close to their own history to create the knockout announcement they needed. Ken White + Associates devised an intricate, interlocking folder that waxes visually and verbally poetic on "time" and "change." Like other White promos, this one demands both tactile and mental involvement as the reader opens its seemingly endless construction. Art director: Ken White; designer: Lisa Levin

## SOFT IMPRESSIONS

*Belyea Design
Seattle, Washington*

Designer Patricia Belyea takes the best of what we think of as "feminine" in design and uses it to her own and her clients' advantage. Her business papers, for example, are muted tones of pink and gray, with her studio signature engraved in a delicate flourish. This system also includes a customized Rolodex card that, in addition to the raves received for her letterhead, has proven a great asset for extra exposure. In a similar vein, promotions for Impression Northwest display that printer's capabilities in modest, if not intimate, terms. The first of these, a set of illustrated bookmarks tucked into a folder that is embellished with poems, was specifically designed to be too special to be thrown away. A delight to virtually all who received them, the sets were in constant demand from the printer's sales reps. This success led to a second, related promotion—illustrated bookplates.

▲ *"Armchair Travel" bookplates for Impression Northwest*

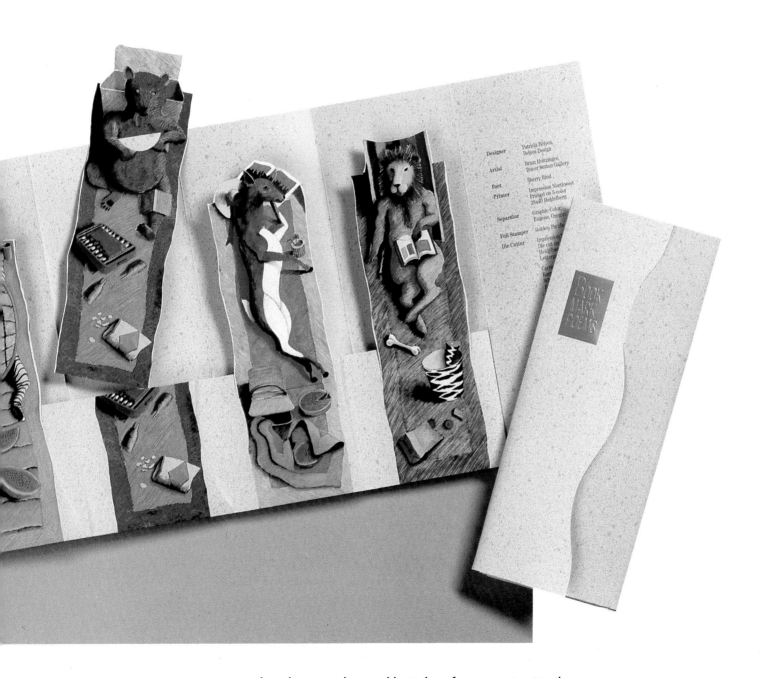

Designer    Patricia Belyea, Belyea Design

Artist    Brian Holtzinger, Traver Sutton Gallery

Poet    Sherry Rind

Printer    Impression Northwest Printed on 5-color 28x40 Heidelberg

Separator    Graphic Color, Eugene, Oregon

Foil Stamper    Golden Pacific

Die Cutter    Impression

▲ *Bookmark-poems designed by Belyea for Impression Northwest*

## REMEMBER THE ALAMO

*Michelle Friesenhahn*
*Design*
*San Antonio, Texas*

San Antonio designer Michelle Friesenhahn struck a responsive chord when she sent the local media and prospective clientele her capabilities brochure for the bogus firm "Alamos `R' Us." Dedicated to "developing the Alamo symbol into innovative visuals sure to enhance [a] company's image," the parody firm displays dozens of successful adaptations of the Alamo's famed silhouette to every conceivable application—from pet pastries and flooring to coathangers, shoes, and "Alamoo" ice cream. While Friesenhahn intended the piece to simply raise her firm's profile in its marketplace, the booklet received lots of media attention and generated numerous requests for the booklet, which ultimately brought in four new accounts. Total cost of the promotion was fifty-five hundred dollars for twenty-five hundred copies.

▲ *Cover and spreads from Friesenhahn's brochure*
*for bogus design firm, "Alamos `R' Us"; booklet measures 5¹/₂ x 11*

# A LIGHT TOUCH

*Tracy Sabin*
*Illustration & Design*
*San Diego, California*

When designer/illustrator Tracy Sabin moved quarters, he needed two things—an attractive moving announcement and new stationery. Sabin saw these as opportunities to put his light and graceful illustration style into the hands of current and prospective clients. Produced for a total cost of eighteen hundred dollars for composites and printing of one thousand copies of each piece, Sabin's new stationery has brought many positive comments—and the moving announcement has brought him all of his mail.

▲ *Tracy Sabin's stationery package*

## Gordon Screen Printing

Sabin's ongoing calendar series for Gordon Screen Printing is aimed at creating a quality image for this San Diego-area shop. Prior to 1985, Sabin had created calendar images of various subjects, such as flowers and beautiful women. That year, however, his "Bogart" calendar brought such response that he and the client decided to pursue the movie-star subject. "Clients and potential customers now view the calendars as collectors' items," Sabin says, "and their inclusion in local and national shows has enhanced the company's profile."

▲ Sabin's moving announcement

▲ Sabin's "movie-star" calendar series for Gordon Screen Printing (also on the following page)

## CELEBRATIONS

*Taylor & Browning
Design Associates
Toronto, Ontario, Canada*

Taylor & Browning Design Associates of Toronto have found self-promotion pieces a good way to celebrate its services. The 1987-88 holiday season also marked the studio's fifth anniversary; partners Scott Taylor and Paul Browning produced a special "T&B" wine package. Filled with a vintage as old as the firm, the bottle was sent in a coordinating setup box to officers at specific client corporations. A few months later, the firm decided not to take its usual two-week summer hiatus; this fact was announced to clients and key suppliers with a "Heatwave 88" T-shirt and postcard mailing. The two promotions had two distinct results: the first, and more elegant, promoted an attitude about the quality of the firm's design and brought phone calls and letters from virtually everyone who received it; the package was also shown in an international packaging magazine. The second, more light-hearted promotion heralded what turned out to be the hottest summer on record—though the designers take no responsibility for that—making the promotion, especially the copywriting, particularly appropriate.

▲ Taylor & Browning's holiday/anniversary wine bottle promotion.
Hang-tag reads, "Taylor & Browning, vintners of fine design since 1982,
would like to join you in celebrating the holiday with a bottle from the
vintners of St. Emilion. May it delight your palette this 1987 season"

▲ "Heatwave 88" T-shirt promotion. Enclosed postcard reads, "Too hot to stop:

This year at Taylor & Browning Design Associates, you'll find us in the heat of the action all summer long"

## A CUT ABOVE

*Stephen Alcorn
Cambridge, New York*

Each year, linocut artist Stephen Alcorn gathers together his recent work and with the assistance of his father, designer John Alcorn, forms them into a new promotion piece. Produced on donated paper and printed in trade, these posters and mailers provide both the artist and the print shop with a dramatic and stylistically unique promotion. For Alcorn, they also bring clients—art directors at studios, agencies, galleries, and presses—up to date on new developments in his work. And, by presenting his work on appropriate stock and in their own context (Alcorn avoids mass-marketed illustration directories), he feels these economical promotions can best display his range of moods and subjects. Moreover, they are indispensable in getting his work before his public and satisfying requests for samples when he is being considered for a specific job. "When a client only has a vague familiarity with my work," he notes, "these prints reinforce that familiarity and clinch the sale."

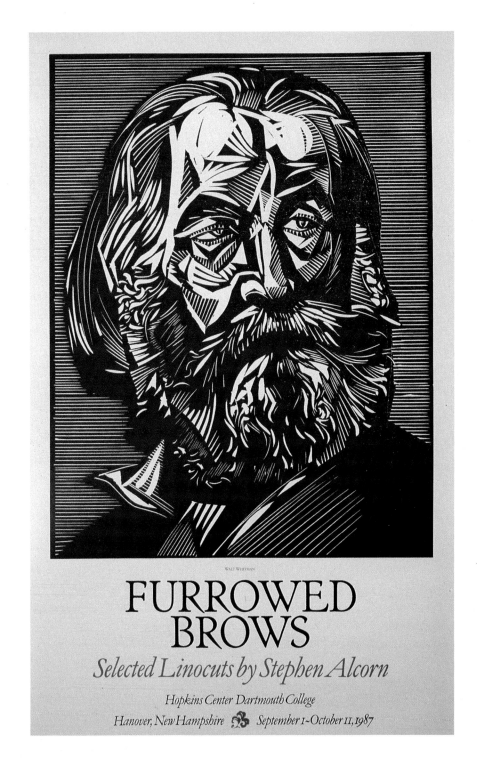

WALT WHITMAN

# FURROWED BROWS

*Selected Linocuts by Stephen Alcorn*

Hopkins Center Dartmouth College

Hanover, New Hampshire   September 1–October 11, 1987

▲ *Poster/promotion for show of Alcorn's work at Dartmouth College.*

*Print shows and sales are an important goal of his promotion strategy*

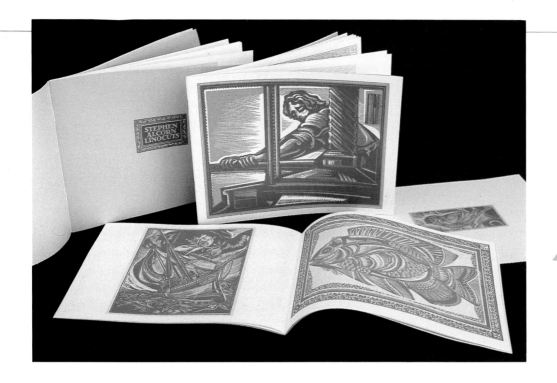

▲ Twenty-four-page, 8 1/2 x 11 brochure illustrates color lino-print technique developed by Stephen Alcorn

▲ Poster announcing programs sponsored by the Connecticut Art Directors Club was a collaborative effort between father, designer John Alcorn (one of the featured speakers), and son: John did the decorative border, Stephen the linocut

## WACKY DOES IT

*Tharp Did It*
*Los Gatos, California*

At Rick Tharp's Tharp Did It studio, self-promotion is a way of life. With few exceptions, Tharp executes his self-promotion in black and white, giving all his pieces a recognizable theme and reflecting the color scheme of his studio. To add personality to Tharp's ongoing campaign, each piece is created around a particular point of parody—a ploy that Tharp hopes will remind his clients that working with him is fun. Although it's difficult for Tharp to place a dollar figure on the revenue that his self-promotion has earned his studio, Tharp believes his unified approach creates a memorable image among his clients—the result being frequent repeat business.

▲ *Tharp rarely misses an opportunity to promote his design services. The mini-billboard (top left) was produced full scale for a radio station but sent in miniature to clients; cost was absorbed by the radio station, whose management liked the minis enough to give them to their sales force. Above are tearsheets of Tharp's work, which Tharp sends to existing and potential clients with a hang-tag and staff photo*

▲ Smaller black-and-white and three-dimensional promotion pieces are seldom issued without a gag. Clockwise, from left:
A holiday Tabasco parody (which one restaurateur put out on the table); announcement card for exhibit of Rick Tharp's
visual puns; Thanksgiving card inviting recipient to save a turkey and "Put another shrimp on the barbie, mate"; "World's
Worst Graphic Designer" postcard, sent to clients who reject Tharp's ideas (including the flight to Paris, this promotion
cost $5,240); five-inch square booklet showing ten years of Tharp-designed logos and marks. Cost: $850 for five hundred

▲ *Tharp Did It rubber stamps both entertain and inform.*

*Says Tharp, "Clients say they enjoy getting mail from us, even if it's a bill"*

▲ *Weymouth Design's brochure amasses over-runs of*

*color sections from fourteen Weymouth-designed annual reports*

## CORPORATE STYLE

*Weymouth Design, Inc.*
*Boston, Massachusetts*

Among those who know corporate annual report design, Weymouth Design, Inc., has a national reputation as creators of corporate communications with a fresh new look. Integral to the firm's success is its ability to provide complete photographic services for the reports it designs. Recent promotions from Weymouth Design play up these facts. A hefty perfect-bound brochure, appropriately titled "Fourteen," uses over-runs of colors sections from fourteen Weymouth-designed annuals, many of which were photographed by Weymouth himself, to prove a point: Weymouth Design knows how to be innovative within an acceptable corporate mode. Supporting this thesis, too, has been a series of ads appearing in a nationally distributed annual report design sourcebook. In both cases, production expenses were minimal—the cost of space for the ads, the cost of printing divider and credit pages and of binding for the brochure. By careful planning and ample forethought, Weymouth has achieved an impressive promotion system that looks more expensive than it is.

## PICTURE THIS

*Andrea Eberbach*
*Indianapolis, Indiana*

In years past, illustrator Andrea Eberbach garnered most of her commissions via a series of color-printed illustrations, tucked in an envelope and sent to prospective clients. In 1989, however, Eberbach changed her tack by collecting the illustrations and creating a more comprehensive pamphlet. The new format both shows off her illustration style and gives Eberbach space to include a brief text describing her relationship to her work. While the earlier efforts were successful, Eberbach says the pamphlet has brought unprecedented numbers of inquiries, as well as better-paying and more interesting assignments. The reason? Perhaps because the words have given her pictures a context, helping clients understand Eberbach's artistic motivation.

▲ *Series of individual, color-printed illustration postcards, measuring 5¹/₂ x 8¹/₂*

▲ *Front and back of Eberbach's most recent promotional pamphlet, measuring 9¹/₄ x 5¹/₄*

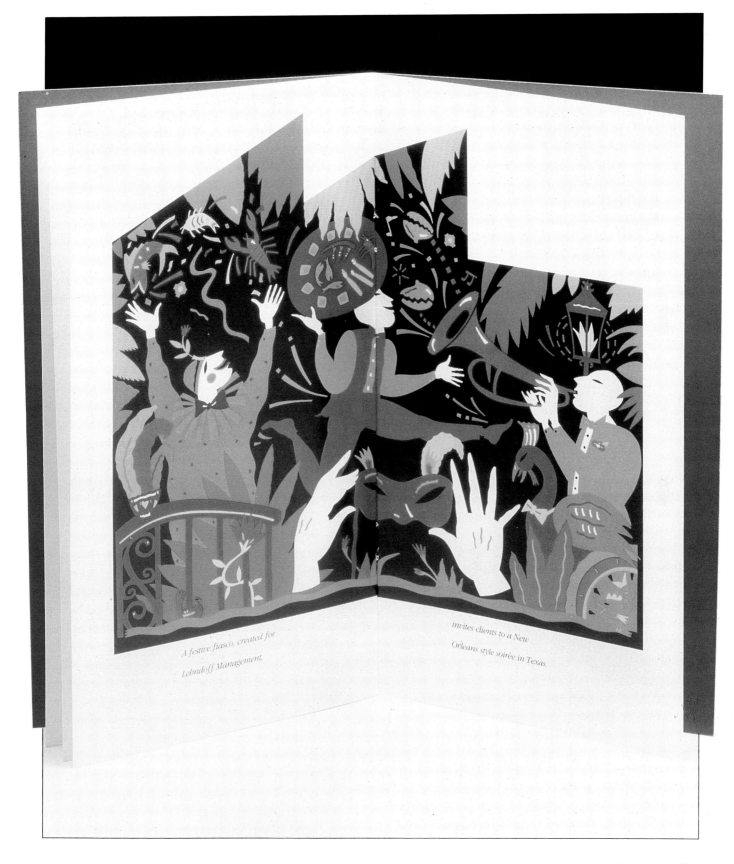

A festive fiasco, created for
Lehndoff Management,

invites clients to a New
Orleans style soirée in Texas.

▲ *Interior spread from pamphlet*

## THE LUCK O' IRISH DESIGN

*The Dunlavey Studio*
*Sacramento, California*

Promotion from the Dunlavey Studio often stems from the fact that its proprietors' roots are in Ireland. The studio also uses humor to show off its creative design skills. Two favorites are an "Irish paperweight" (in truth, a genuine Idaho potato) and a piece of the Blarney Stone (a bit of colored plastic foam) packed in a Mason jar. Designer Michael Dunlavey even went so far as to create a fictitious Irish ancestor, Cormac, whose dour portrait looks out over the studio and "keeps everyone in line." While it's difficult to measure the exact success of each promotional piece, Michael Dunlavey is confident that his unusual pieces have an impact on clients: "These Blarney Stone jars have been sitting on clients' desks for years."

▲ Irish potato paperweight

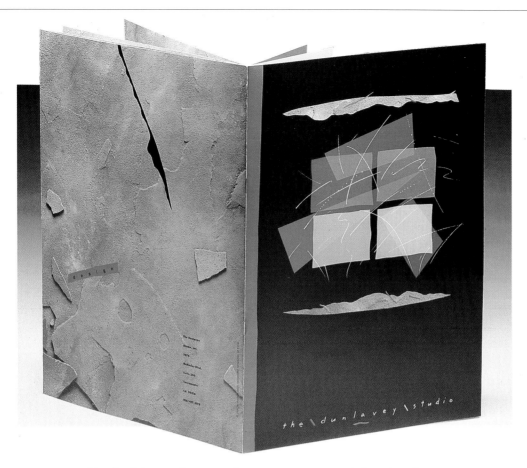

▲ *Cover and back of the Dunlavey Studio's most recent capabilities brochure, measuring 9 x 12¹/₂*

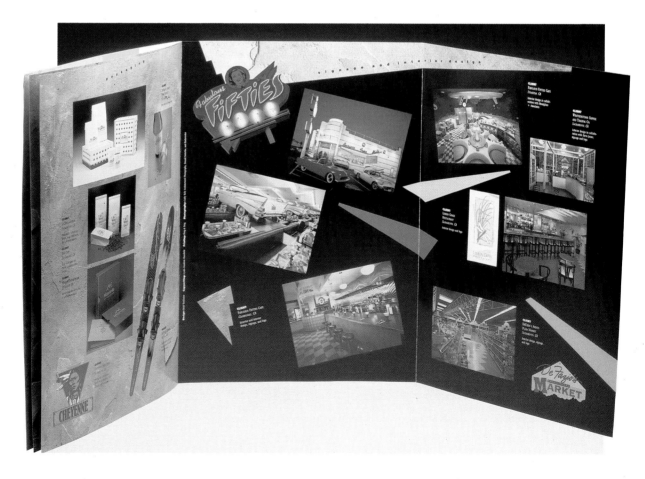

▲ *Interior spread from Dunlavey's brochure*

▲ "When Irish ties are smiling" invitation to Dunlavey Studio's Irish theme party

▲ Blarney stone (plastic foam)

packed in a Mason jar

## CONCEPTUAL CONTEXTS

*Curry Design*
*Los Angeles, California*

For several years, graphic designer Steve Curry has been sending clients a bottle of wine at Christmas. Produced as a joint promotion with a local typographer and a screen printer, Curry donates his design services and in return receives a classy promotion for his own studio. In 1989, Curry added another promotion to the gift-package concept: a set of four cards with a vellum overlay. Printed on both sides, the cards use conceptual art to suggest some of the studio's philosophical bases without getting heavy-handed. This latest promotion has brought an encouraging response from the larger, more upscale clients the studio has been trying to reach.

▲ *Christmas wine sent as gifts to clients of Curry Design*

▲ Conceptual card-mailer for Curry Design. Overlay reads: "Responsible Design goes far beyond what is

simply fashionable. It serves the client, communicates clearly, and solves the problem with style."

Each card also carries a designed message on the reverse —Eye: "We have an eye for detail"

Ear: "We listen 2 your needs"

Mouth: "We speak your language"

Hand: "We can handle your difficult jobs"

▲ Eiber's RED stationery

## SEEING RED

*Rick Eiber Design*
*Seattle, Washington*

Designer Rick Eiber is a firm believer in the old adage, "Where there's a will, there's a way." "Anyone truly committed to producing an exceptional promotion will find people to work with them," he says, "and at very little cost." As proof, he offers promotional pieces produced by his own studio in cooperation with local printers, typographers, and color separators. The centerpiece (shown on the following page), which he estimates would have cost twenty thousand dollars had not all services but paper been donated, offers its producers a chance to show clients their range of expertise. Presented to prospective clients, this book has brought Eiber a high percentage of commissions. In another effort, Eiber designed a series of posters for a local typographer; these, too, brought dramatic response in the form of requests for catalogs and committed orders.

▲ *Capabilities brochure for Rick Eiber Design*

## BLACK MAGIC

*Renee Sullivan*
*Burlingame, California*

Renee Sullivan's presentation folder was designed as an imaging piece. "I needed something that expressed my personality," the designer says, "in a surprising, yet elegant, fashion." Her solution: a three-panel folder to hold correspondence or samples, a notecard, and a calling card, all dramatically designed in black and white. Sullivan reports much enthusiasm from those who have seen the new system—as well as comments as to how aptly it reflects her personality. Moreover, it appears to enhance the presentation of actual works in progress. "After this kind of presentation," she says, "people are much more respectful of your time and talent."

▲ *Designer Renee Sullivan's presentation system*

## A HISTORIC MOVE

*Donovan and Green*
*New York, New York*

When designers Donovan and Green moved to the top of New York's historic Metropolitan Life Tower, they wished to share with their clients—many of whom are architects and real estate developers—some of the wonderful history of both the structure and its area. So they devised an elegant accordion-folded moving announcement, printed on vellum in red and gray and tied with a red ribbon. The piece, which measures twenty-eight inches long when unfolded, not only announces the firm's new location but offers an encapsulated history of the tower and Madison Square. "The announcement brought tremendous response," says principal Nancye Green. "Because it didn't promote Donovan and Green directly, and because the material presented is inherently interesting, it has 'hung around.' We still find it in clients' and friends' offices."

▲ *Donovan and Green announce their move to New York's Metropolitan Life Tower, with "expanded facilities, studios and offices with inspiring views"*

## THINK PIECE

*Frazier Design*
*San Francisco, California*

One of the basic tenets of good design is that it must be founded on a strong concept. Such is the case with Frazier Design's recent promotion, itself a collection of thoughts and ideas about successful graphic communications. Penned by proprietor Craig Frazier and interleaved with photos of successful design projects, the philosophical content of this book neatly qualifies Frazier Design in the minds of prospective clients; those who appreciate the designer's thinking generally call asking for more. And at twenty dollars per wire-bound copy, the book can be easily and economically updated for strategic use as a leave-behind.

▲ *Frazier Design's wire-o book, which opens to a 24 x 15³/₄ spread, combines thoughts about design with successful communications projects*

The secret of

persuasion is

providing meaning.

When was the last time

you were confused into

making up your mind?

The secret to successful business:
Speak your customer's language.

The secret to successful design:
Speak your customer's customer's language.

▲ *Production is low key. Oversize pages are uncoated; quotes and endpapers are rich and glossy*

## NEW WAVE PROMO

*Graffito*
*Baltimore, Maryland*

If the high-energy graphics produced by Graffito must at times be reined in to solve clients' communications problems, the design firm's self-promotion rides far and wide across the New Wave. Most conservative is the firm's one "corporate" piece—a folder with loose inserts. Here rips, spatters, and floating graphics are subtle enough to let the firm's impressive array of successful design projects take the reader's eye. Useful as a send-ahead and leave-behind, the kit cost thirty-five thousand dollars to produce and has brought response far beyond the designers' expectations. Says Graffito art director Tim Thompson, "Some of the country's biggest corporations have praised this package as unique, exciting, and memorable." Still, this promo is fairly tame compared with the posters and other, less formal promotions the firm has done. The first of these, a co-promotion with Graphtec color separators, pushed the studio's technical capabilities at the time "to the max." "This poster really put us on the regional map," says Graffito designer Dave Plunkert. "Response from prospective clients and peers was tremendous, and it easily paid for itself [twenty thousand dollars] in the number of new clients we picked up because of the exposure." A second poster pushed the firm's Lightspeed technology even further with the addition of electronic pre-press techniques.

▲ *Graffito's folder promotion kit with loose-leaf inserts*

▲ Promotion posters, documenting Graffito's skills at the leading edge of technology, landed numerous new accounts

▲ Michael Cronan's "walking man"

symbol, surrounded by other "design quality" symbols on his promotional poster

## SYMBOLIC TRADITIONS

*Michael P. Cronan Design
San Francisco, California*

For years, graphic designer Michael P. Cronan has used as a personal signature a walking-man figure that has achieved considerable recognition, especially among West Coast designers. In addition, Cronan has designed a whole series of symbolic characters, which he uses judiciously and where appropriate, to indicate the major qualities of the graphic communications he produces. By way of more complete explanation, Cronan took the opportunity offered by a speaking engagement before the Omaha Art Directors Club to produce a promotional poster for himself. Here, the central "walking man" is surrounded by the communications-related symbols and words describing their meaning—"utility," for example, or "myth," "artifact," "challenge." Used inconspicuously, like charms, on many of the pieces his studio produces, the graphic symbols are teasers, raising the design consciousness of those who see Cronan's work.

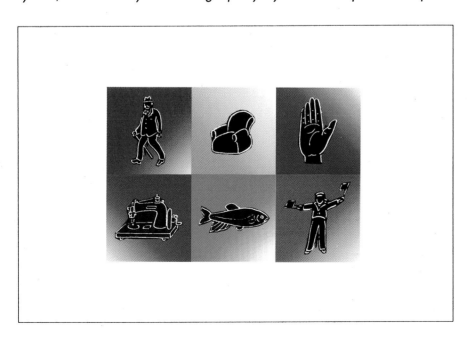

▲ Coordinating Cronan Design notecard

## DUAL DUTY

*The Weller Institute
for the Cure of Design
Park City, Utah*

Don Weller, who with his part-
ner/wife Chikako runs the Weller
Institute for the Cure of Design,
has a knack, as Chikako says, for
"solving his clients' problems and
his own need for self-promotion
at the same time." An artist of
many talents, Weller is often
asked to speak at art directors
clubs and graphic communications societies; his illustrations
show up on posters for these
events, for printers, and for The
Design Conference That Just
Happens to Be In Park City (of
which he was a founder). Promotions like this have built a steady
awareness of his work within the
design community. For his clients
and business prospects, however,
the Wellers created a more serious promotion piece that focuses
only on the Institute's projects.
Originally produced as a trade
agreement with a printer, this
angle-cut folder with loose cards
has proved easy and economical
to update and maintain; new
sheets can be run in the waste
areas of larger jobs, reducing
costs to those of separations and
a small percentage of the printing bill.

▲ *Posters designed by Weller to promote his speaking engagements in
New Mexico and Oklahoma also serve as promotions for his own work*

▲ Loose-leaf portfolio for The Weller Institute for
the Cure of Design measures 4 x 8⁷/₈

▲ Promotion Weller designed and illustrated for Sinclair Printing

▲ Poster for 1989 conference

▲ Poster for 1987 conference

▲ Poster/announcements for annual design conference held in Park City, Utah.
As a founder of the conference, Weller is instrumental in its planning and promotion

▲ *Art Chantry's specialized logotype promotion*

## FABULOUS FUNK

*Art Chantry Design*
*Seattle, Washington*

Whether for himself or for a supplier or colleague, Art Chantry's promotion pieces display all of the creative, if slightly irreverent, talents that have labeled him as one of the most inventive young designers in the Pacific Northwest. His own logotype promotion is a literal case in point. Produced, he says, "to get the word out that I also design peculiar and interesting stylized typographic treatments," this double-sided, translucent plastic poster was sent "reservedly" so as to track its effectiveness. A total of sixty-seven were mailed; about half the recipients responded, of whom Chantry estimates between fifteen and twenty gave him work. His expenses for this promotion were "postage, period." Perhaps most popular—and most unorthodox—have been Chantry's Christmas cards for Mogelgaard & Associates, a Seattle agency itself known for irreverent creativity. These holiday greetings inevitably focus upon Mike Mogelgaard as a personality and rely heavily on parody for their impact. Mogelgaard as Elvis in a red lamé Santa suit or as a sleazy "nice guy" preparing for Christmas. Ranging in cost from postage alone to several dollars per copy, their fiscal effectiveness, Chantry says, is difficult to assess. "No marketing surveys can be done on pieces as insidious as these. The best measure is their continued popularity and the clamor to get on Mike's mailing list."

▲ Chantry's 1986 Christmas greeting for Seattle agency Mogelgaard & Associates parodied Elvis
    Presley's "50,000,000 Elvis Fans Can't Be Wrong" album cover. Inside is an attached transparent record of
        Mike Mogelgaard singing "Blue Christmas." Says Chantry, "I love the idea of Mike spinning around on your turntable"

Mogelgaard's 1988 "Advent Calendar" holiday card is meant to be mounted in a window. Roughly produced from card stock and vellum, six small doors on the front open to reveal translucent images of Mogelgaard caught up in the spirit of Christmas

An extension of the previous year's "Elvis" greeting, the 1987 Mogelgaard card was a montage of Mogelgaard's face with those of authentic fifties rock-and-rollers. From a loosely pencilled layout, a showcard company assembled the elements using wooden type and copper engravings of halftone art. "This was intended to be mailed as a giant Christmas postcard," says Chantry, "but the post office made us put it into an envelope."

## PROMO, WITH HEART

*Rickabaugh Graphics*
*Columbus, Ohio*

At Rickabaugh Graphics, every piece that leaves the studio is seen as promotion, giving life to the saying that a designer is only as good as his or her last job. What self-promotion the studio does produce, however, reflects warmth and friendliness and not a little grace. While the Christmas holidays offer the firm a yearly opportunity to produce something special, other occasions also occur—the birth of proprietor Eric Rickabaugh's daughter, for example, or the creation of a studio bowling team. The designer even created a set of decorative rubber stamps so as to personalize pieces of communication. And, because the studio does a substantial number of pro bono and low-budget work for arts and other community-service organizations, a stamp-like "Labor of Love" logo was created to identify those jobs. When this particular design immediately brought a year's worth of pro bono assignments, Rickabaugh was not dismayed: such jobs put his work into places his mailing list doesn't reach and, he believes, have much more impact than would a stilted capabilities brochure. With as much as a third of the studio's assignments being generated by pro bono or self-promotion work, Rickabaugh may well be right.

▲ Christmas wine, sent to clients, suppliers, and friends of Rickabaugh

Graphics, offered "something to make yourself a little holiday toast"

Within the Christmas card image:

YOUR FRIENDS
AT RICKABAUGH
GRAPHICS WISH
YOU AND YOURS
A VERY MERRY

AND WE HOPE
YOUR COMING
NEW YEAR IS
FULL OF LOVE
& GOOD CHEER!

▲ *Rickabaugh Graphics Christmas card*

▲ *Logo for pro bono work produced by Rickabaugh Graphics*

▲ Rickabaugh's logo and brochure for Columbus Typographics promotes their desktop type business with

"important dates in the history of type," which include Columbus sailing the wide "C's" in search of India,

the discovery of X-rays, B-movies, and—of course—Columbus Typographics' desktop output

## SMILE STYLE

*Sibley Peteet Design*
*Dallas, Texas*

"Graphic design is hard work," says Rex Peteet of Sibley Peteet Design. For this reason, he and his partner, Don Sibley, try to have fun with their self-promotions—even the more serious ones. "We're more casual than many firms," adds Sibley, "despite our corporate clients. There's a lot of humor in the studio, and this is reflected in our promotion." But while the firm's promotions are bright and lighthearted, they avoid puns and slapstick solutions for a graphic look that is more high-style. Costs are kept to a minimum by trading out services to suppliers. Their logo book—a wire-bound showcase tucked inside a glossy, interlocking die-cut package—was printed at cost and comprises the designers' most ambitious effort; it's made the difference, says Peteet, in landing several new accounts. And the fact that self-promotion design is wide open plugs into the firm's greater strategy for exposure: Designed with awards and shows in mind, these mailers, when published, can ultimately be seen by fifty thousand people, many of them prospective clients.

▲ Sibley Peteet logo book

▲ Salt and pepper posters were printed as overruns from announcements for speaking engagements at the Tulsa and Omaha art directors clubs. The first initiates the "S&P" partnership metaphor; the second, by virtue of a computer-generated illustration, alludes to the firm's addition of computers to their design process

▲ *Sibley Peteet movable Christmas card*

▲ *A stylish necessity, Sibley Peteet's moving announcement*

*made creative use of inks and varnish; was framed and*

*hung by several clients, creating an ongoing promotion*

## SUPPLY-SIDE PROMO

*Sullivan Perkins Design*
*Dallas, Texas*

The designer/copywriter team of Ron Sullivan and Mark Perkins has found that solid relationships with local graphic arts suppliers can lead to fun assignments— and ease their own promotion budget. The firm's annual Christmas greeting is a case in point. Two recent mailers, a twenty-page collection of Christmas anecdotes and a 9" x 38" poster, were both produced at no cost— all materials and production were donated. Both brought positive response from clients and friends. In return, Sullivan Perkins also welcomes the opportunity to help their suppliers promote their own businesses. The posters shown here, executed for a printer and a color separator, offer proof positive of their clients' quality services.

▲ *High-style posters for Artesian Press announce*

*a move and invite to a party. In each, surface texture is*

*created through imaginative use of inks and varnishes*

▲ Holiday greetings from Sullivan Perkins. Booklet features

charming anecdotes and sayings pertinent to the gift-giving season

▲ A poster for Harper House color separators promotes the sophistication of the client's business

## "GIFTED" CLIENTS

*Warkulwiz Design
Associates
Philadelphia, Pennsylvania*

Bob Warkulwiz, Bill Smith, and Mike Rogalski—partners in Warkulwiz Design Associates— see the Christmas holidays as an occasion to send a little something to their clients. For the last decade, this annual promotion has caught the spirit of the season with a small plastic gift, guaranteed to bring good cheer. Sometime after Thanksgiving each year, the partners engage in a bit of brainstorming, which may be assisted by a catalog of advertising specialty products. The point is to devise a witty, text-and-image gag that delights recipients and presents Warkulwiz Design as a multitalented group also capable of having fun. To keep costs down, the firm restricts their holiday mailing list to around seven hundred, despite constant requests for inclusion; each piece costs between one and two dollars to produce. The three-dimensional puns have been so successful that, when the firm moved to new offices, a similar gag gift went out as a moving announcement—a pair of wind-up plastic feet.

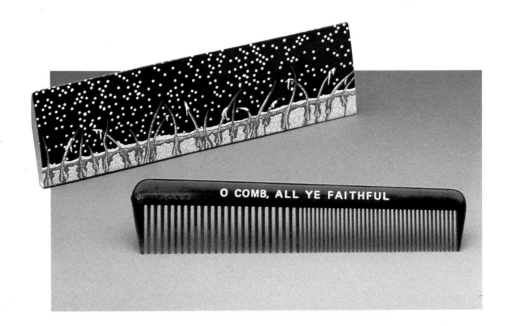

▲ *"O comb, all ye faithful" promotion brings "holiday greetings*

*from those heads-up folks" at Warkulwiz Design*

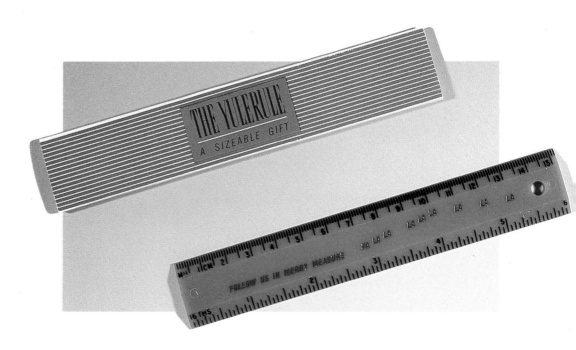

▲ *"The Yule Rule—A Sizable Gift" invites clients to "follow us in merry measure"*

▲ "Insta-Trim Capsules" containing sponge tree ornaments
promise to help clients spruce up their holidays

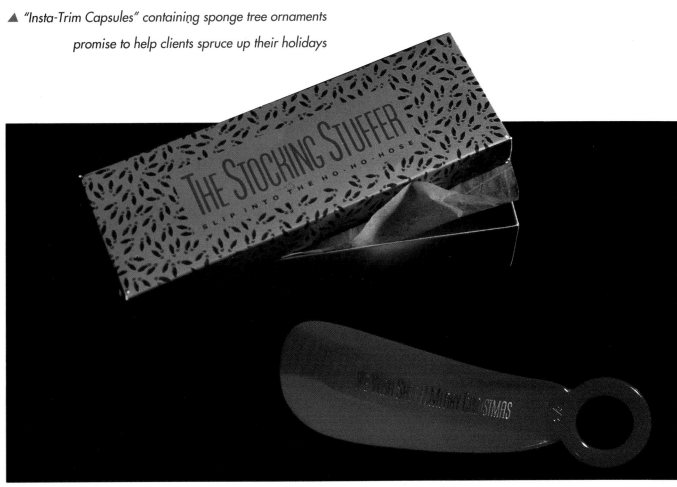

▲ Elegant holiday box holds another plastic gift—a red shoehorn that says, "We Wish Shoe a Merry Christmas."
Designers report this gift really helped them get a foot in the door with a few new clients

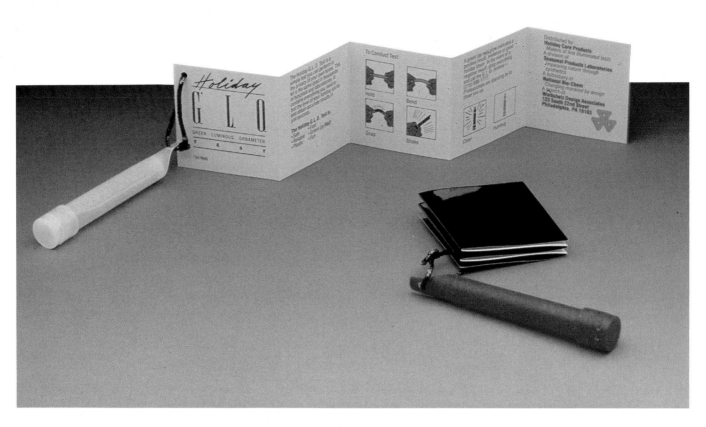

▲ Parodying home pregnancy test kits, the "Holiday Glo Test" measures recipient's cheer level.

In case of negative result, the designers provided a GLO Hotline,

which they say was busy for several months after the mailing

▲ Warkulwiz Design's moving announcement

literally walked into recipients' hands. People are still talking about it

▲ Alling and Cory paper show invitation

*It's finally arrived...*

▲ Brochure introducing new premium-grade gloss paper for U.S. market

## Paper Magic/Ikonofix Gloss Promos

And on a more serious note, Warkulwiz Design Associates' promotions for paper manufacturers meet specific client needs with individual style. The "Paper Magic" exhibition announcement utilizes the translucent nature of parchment to suggest a sleight of hand; attendance of that event was far greater than expected, and the job brought more promo work from the client. The full-color, gate-fold promotion for Zanders' new Ikonofix Gloss sheet sparked orders and generated calls from designers nationwide about both the paper and the printing.

## SERIOUS STRATEGIES

*The Graphic Expression
New York, New York*

Corporate designers at The Graphic Expression produce promotions in which their top-level corporate clients speak for them. Their first promotion, two books created separately but mailed together in a coordinating folder, employs first- and third-person case histories of successful corporate communications projects. These illustrate the importance of superior communications in indicating corporate leadership. These volumes were later enhanced with a third thought-piece that, again using the clients' own words, speaks to some of the issues on the minds of corporate communicators today. This serious, corporate focus, consistently expressed, has strategically positioned The Graphic Expression as a design studio that thinks like, and is therefore responsive to, businesses they serve.

▲ *Corporate communications strategies from The Graphic Expression*

▲ Superior communications indicate corporate leadership

in this promotional book produced by the Graphic Expression

## WATERMULLINS

*Paul Mullins Associates*
*Fresno, California*

Watermelons hold a particular fascination for designer Paul Mullins, so much so that he has adopted the fruit as a studio symbol. When he recently moved to a new office, Mullins created a serigraph print of a "Watermullin," suitable for framing, and sent it out in a Mullin-like tube. A vellum overlay carried pertinent information so as not to spoil the Mullin. The poster was followed by a Christmas tree ornament in the shape of a slice of Watermullin, decorated in tinsel, like a miniature tree. Both promotions were produced at very little cost—the silkscreen prints were made in a back room of Mullins's office; the Mullin-tree was cut from wood, painted and decorated by Mullins's staff; the tag came from an instant printer. These first Watermullin promotions so firmly linked the studio with the fruit that two more are in the offing: a Watermullin jack-o-lantern (for Halloween, of course) and a bird's nest with a tiny Watermullin egg.

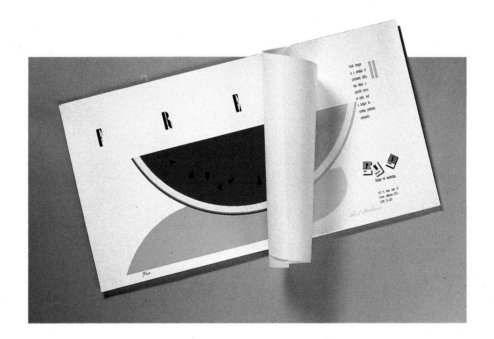

▲ *Paul Mullins Associates "Watermullin" promotions*
*have gained the studio new awareness, are continually*
*building image among clients and colleagues*

## CHANGING COURSES

*Sabina Fascione Alcorn*
*Cambridge, New York*

Sabina Fascione Alcorn once made her living as a textile designer, but the flat, stylized designs of that craft left her unfulfilled. Her real satisfaction came from the paintings she did for herself—watercolors, made from observation, in the style of the eighteenth-century French botanical illustrators. She longed to make these soul-felt works her source of income, but how to make the switch? Following the lead of her husband (artist Stephen Alcorn) and father-in-law (designer John Alcorn), she made a deal with fine photography printer Morgan Press: her illustrations in return for some poster/promotion pieces. The flower poster was particularly successful, and in an unexpected way: framed and hung in a major upstate New York nursery, the calendar was seen by a woman already writing a book on celebrated American gardens. She tracked Sabina down, and the illustrator soon signed a contract with Clarkson Potter to illustrate the book.

▲ *Sabina Fascione Alcorn's illustrated calendars for fine printer Morgan Press*
*announced new color printing equipment. They brought the printer orders, the*
*illustrator a major assignment, and both individual-copy sales.*

## SPECIAL ISSUES

*Richards Brock Miller Mitchell and Associates
Dallas, Texas*

The Richards Brock Miller Mitchell Christmas greeting is the only significant self-promotion the firm does all year and for employees it takes on a special significance. Each designer in the firm is responsible for producing at least one idea, as time allows. Then, as the season draws near, all meet as a group to discuss and vote on the issue. The winner gets to produce his or her idea. By trading services with printers, costs for producing the annual seven hundred to one thousand posters are kept low. On one rare occasion, a specific need for a promotion piece arose. Because of the firm's link through principal Stan Richards with a top ad agency in town, many advertising art directors did not know that RBMM also had a separate and autonomous film production unit, headed by principal Ed Brock. A poster reinforcing that fact utilized "motion" photography to suggest the firm's forte—animation design. Mailed to some eight hundred art directors and designers in agencies and studios in the Dallas area, the poster promotion clearly met its goal: It not only increased awareness of Brock Films within the target audience; since its dissemination, Brock says, his film business has landed jobs with every agency in town.

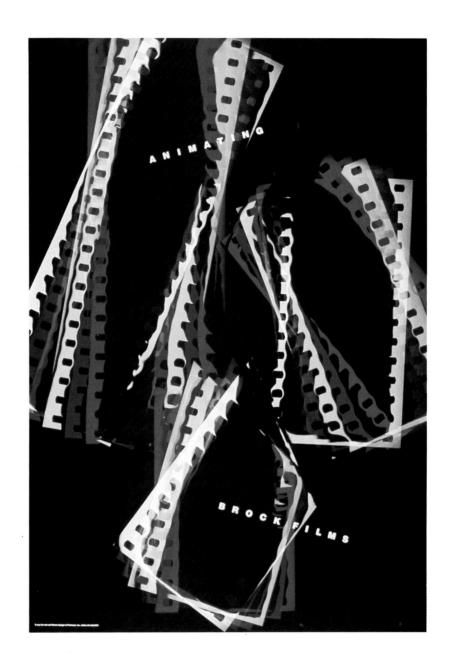

▲ *Poster promotion for Brock Films, animators*

▲ Christmas posters/promotions from Richards Brock Miller Mitchell and Associates

## BRIGHT IMAGES

*Bright & Associates
New York, New York, and
Los Angeles, California*

Bi-coastal identity and design consultants Bright & Associates uses a handsome but friendly promotion kit to support the efforts of its sales and public relations staff. The cornerstone of the kit is a periwinkle blue folder, lined with golden yellow, that serves as a presentation device for press releases, promotional materials, or job proposals. The coordination of this folder with other key ingredients—8$^1$/$_2$" x 11" job case history cards, for example, or business papers also backed with blue—substantiates Bright & Associates' claimed expertise as an image-creating design firm. By printing a few thousand at a time, both folders and mailers can be .frequently updated. But perhaps Bright's best-tasting goody is the one given to prospects at the end of the presentation—a periwinkle blue box filled with chocolates molded into the shapes of corporate symbols designed by the firm. "Our self-promotion isn't meant to work out of context," cautions firm president Keith Bright. "Our work alone makes us credible. Still, promotion like this can make the difference between making a sale or not."

▲ Bright & Associates' Christmas card spoofs their own trade with identity standards for "S. Claus Enterprises." Designer: Randall Hensley

▲ At a cost of ten to fifteen dollars per copy, Bright & Associates' colorful promotion kit is used to support personal sales presentations

▲ Issues of the eminently successful series, "Annual Report Trends,"
designed by John Cleveland for the S.D. Warren paper company

## Promotions for S.D. Warren

One of the accounts that came to Bright & Associates with the acquisition of John Cleveland, Inc., was a continuing promotion effort for the S.D. Warren Company. For four years, Cleveland had designed the paper company's premier selling effort to the elite annual report paper specifying market, "Annual Report Trends." Besides gaining recognition for the designer, this series through the years has brought important information to Warren's primary customers. As the only promotion produced by the company on an annual basis (there have been nine editions thus far), its longevity is proof of its success, both in creating demand for Warren papers and in meeting a marketing strategy based on education. Aimed at an entirely different buyer, Cleveland worked with consultants in direct response marketing Brooster and Associates Unlimited to create a different kind of educational promotion—the "Handbook of Direct Response Production." While Warren's manager of advertising and marketing services, Corby Saunders, characterizes both the "Trends" series and the handbook as "tremendously successful pieces," the direct response to promotion set something of a response record itself—some 120,000 copies of the handbook were requested within its first two months of publication.

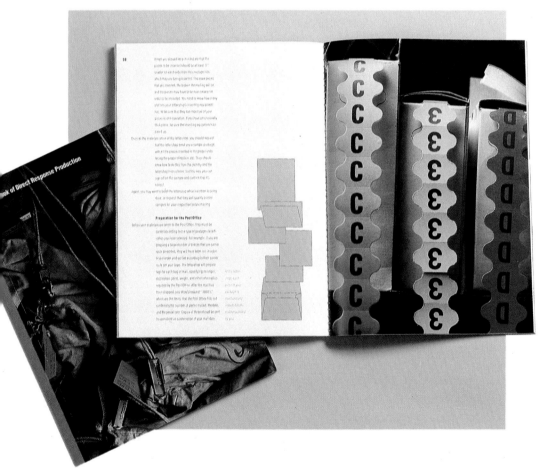

▲ Another Warren promotion designed by Cleveland aims at the burgeoning
direct-mail market with a three-part campaign, builds new market base
for the client with multiple mailings

## FIRST IMPRESSION

*Corporate Graphics Inc.
New York, New York;
Los Angeles, California,
and London, England*

The primary promotion piece for Corporate Graphics Inc is an oversized, squarish (10$^1$/$_2$" x 11") brochure produced economically with reproduction materials from corporate communications designed by the firm. The twenty-page brochure finds greatest use in creating awareness of CGI's capabilities in new markets. Based in New York, CGI recently opened offices in Los Angeles and London. In these untapped areas, as Los Angeles head Steve Martin explains, large numbers of potential clients needed to be reached, and a few hundred work samples simply wouldn't suffice. "When you need to make your presence known," says Martin, "a brochure allows you to cover a broad geographical base. We can introduce ourselves and make an impression on a lot of different desks, then follow up with samples if there's real interest." The brochure is used as a reminder after the firm has made a proposal, continuing the impression through the time it takes a client to reach a decision, and is distributed to attendees at conferences and seminars where CGI principals are invited to speak.

▲ *Corporate Graphic Inc's promotional brochure was formatted to make use of separations and negatives from corporate communications designed for clients*

## GRAND OPENING

*Diagram Design
and Marketing
Communications, Inc.
New York, New York*

One of the most difficult jobs a designer can attempt is creating an image for his or her own studio. When Diana Graham started her own graphic design firm, she faced just such a challenge. She began with a name she very much wanted to use— "Diagram," an amalgam of her own name and incidentally suggestive of another quality design firm. And she knew she wanted not just a typographic solution, but a logo-mark—a name-shape that would be distinctive. "Most designers use a logo but not consistently," Graham says. "I wanted a logo to use forever, not only as a name but as a logo-type—something symbolic, that was appropriate because of my involvement with type." From the outset, this Diagram logo has been consistently applied—on stationery, greeting cards, capabilities brochures—wherever the studio name appears. Besides bringing her firm awards and peer recognition, the identity has succeeded in creating a strong image for her company. As her business has grown, Graham has produced a second capabilities book specifically aimed at annual report clients. Still, her original promotion proves to be a very valuable tool. Says Graham, "It brings in projects and more clients."

▲ *"Openings" booklet announces the opening of Diagram Design*

▲ *Diagram's original capabilities brochure is still a valuable selling tool*

▲ *Diagram promotion/folder aimed at annual report clients*

▲ *Diagram Valentine, sent to new clients, casts logotype in pure chocolate*

## ACES HIGH

*Gunn Associates*
*Boston, Massachusetts*

With more than thirty years in the business, graphic and industrial designers Gunn Associates has an established reputation to uphold. The firm's self-promotion system, which was designed both to increase sales of quality assignments and recognition of the Gunn name, utilizes presentation folders and brochures with four different playing-card covers. While covers and inside photography change, text remains constant in detailing the firm's design philosophy. "The program has exceeded expectations," says Gunn's president and treasurer, David Lizotte. "Sales have increased 10 percent per year over our previous performance." In addition, the manufacturer of the paper used in the brochure distributed five hundred copies internationally as a paper promotion, resulting in calls and letters from many parts of the world.

▲ *Gunn Associates' promotional system features oversized (8 x 13) folders and brochures with embossed, hot-foil stamped covers. Five thousand were printed at a cost of nine dollars per copy.*

## Promotions for Nimrod

This luxurious "metal"-fronted brochure for Nimrod Press aimed at establishing Nimrod as an extraordinary printer, capable of doing some of the best printing in the United States. Its designer, David Lizotte of Gunn Associates, reports that the book achieved excellent results as an image-builder and a moderate increase in printing sales. Interestingly, of the two covers used, "steel" and "copper," the copper proved more popular.

▲ *Forty-eight-page promotional brochure for Nimrod Press, designed by Gunn Associates, shows off the firm's printing and engraving expertise. Ten thousand copies were printed at a total cost of seventy-five thousand dollars*

## PORTABLE PORTFOLIO

*Hixo, Inc.*
*Austin, Texas, and*
*Santa Monica, California*

Before graphic designer Mike Hicks, of Hixo, Inc., put together his capabilities brochure, new-client presentations were oftentimes awkward—a few samples hastily pulled together, a slide show in unpredictable conditions. With the brochure, however, he reports a new ease in reaching prospects. First introduced via a business reply card that lands him a meeting with a potential client, the brochure allows him to personally talk through a sampling of his recent graphic design projects. Then, if the new client is interested, the book can be left behind for further study. Hicks found this method especially successful in developing business for a new office opened in Santa Monica, California. "The brochure has great pass-on value," he says. "I can now be in places I wouldn't have been before." But perhaps more significant is the resultant change in his image among corporate prospects. "A color brochure makes corporate people more comfortable," he adds. "Printed material has more credibility, and is seen as more businesslike. It's a great boon to corporate bonding."

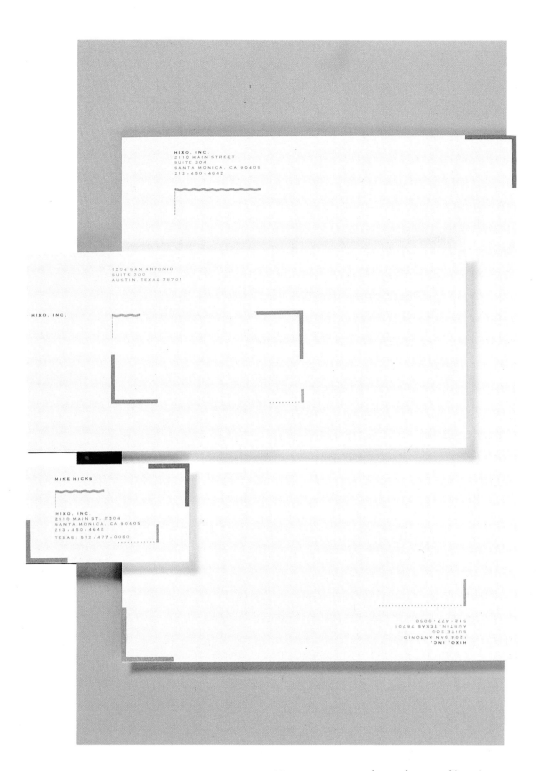

▲ *Hixo stationery echoes design of brochure*

▲ *At a cost of nearly twenty dollars per copy, Hixo's capabilities book is used for one-on-one new-client presentations. Its spiral binding allows for easy updating and editing*

## SEEING DOUBLE

*The Duffy Design Group*
*Minneapolis, Minnesota*

Two promotions from the spirited Duffy Design Group serve two masters—the designers and the French Paper Company. The first piece graphically suggests to designers "what's possible" on French's Speckletone paper, by showing the Duffy group's work on the line. The second and companion piece promotes new Speckletone colors. Together the books sport a host of production techniques, from lithography and thermography to die-cutting, engraving, and foil-stamping, to gate-folds, short sheets, and wire-o binding. While Duffy reports that the paper company spent around eighty thousand dollars for each book, the design firm spent countless hours—and in return received two handsome promotions for their own work. "Speckletone went from number six to number one on French Paper's roster within six months of distribution of the first book," says its co-designer, Joseph Duffy. "French had to drop four paper lines in order to keep up with demand for paper among graphic designers." The second book, he adds, successfully extended the Speckletone line and added significantly to sales. Moreover, "The first book," he says, "was a very successful new business promo for Duffy Design Group, and the second became a valuable capabilities extension."

▲ The Duffy Design Group's double promotion for Speckletone from French Paper
(also shown on facing page) brought attention to both client and designer

▲ *The paper promotions feature work by the Duffy Group, in a variety of production techniques*

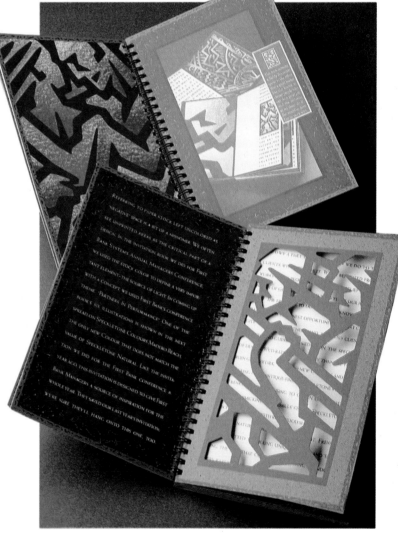

## SWEET FIFTEEN

*Bernhardt Fudyma*
*Design Group*
*New York, New York*

Graphic designers Bernhardt Fudyma Design Group had never done any formal promotion of their services, but as the firm's fifteenth anniversary approached, its principals, Craig Bernhardt and Janice Fudyma, thought a printed commemoration might be in order. They planned an intriguing, highly conceptual booklet that calls to mind all that the last fifteen years has added to our lives—things like "smurfs," "Reeboks," "artificial hearts," "J.R.," and many more. Accompanying art and photography feature visual summations of the magic number— bowling shoes sized $7^1/_2$, for example. As the principals began press planning, they discovered that the press sheet had room for another fourteen pages. They quickly prepared a series of more straightforward project case histories, which they mailed as a follow-up booklet about two weeks after the first. Response to the booklets has been encouraging, with numerous calls and letters and at least one job directly resulting. The mailing was also picked up for documentation in a major graphics magazine. The designers are so pleased with the results of this effort that they have changed their minds about self-promotion. "We're now planning a series of booklets on specific areas of expertise—annual reports, corporate identity, house organs," Bernhardt says. "All will fit into the same square, `family' format."

▲ *Bernhardt Fudyma's fifteenth-anniversary promotion, comprised of a conceptual book on "fifteen years" and a second highlighting major projects*

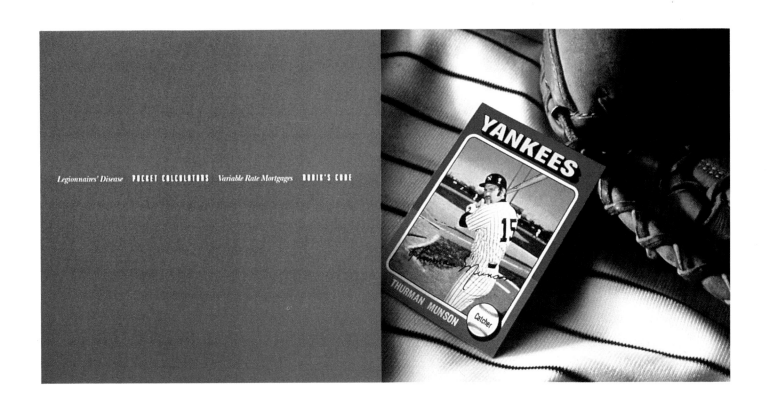

Legionnaires' Disease  POCKET CALCULATORS  *Variable Rate Mortgages*  RUBIK'S CUBE

*Push Thru Tabs On Cans*  THE END  *Crack*  YUPPIES  *Video Cassette Recorders*  J.R.

▲ Spreads from Bernhardt Fudyma's fifteenth-anniversary booklet.

Text highlights additions to our lives in the last fifteen years

## COMIC POWER

*The Dynamic Duo Studio
New York, New York*

Comic artists Arlen Schumer and
Sherri Wolfgang, who bill themselves as the Dynamic Duo, be-
lieve that the potential of comic
art in advertising and editorial
illustration has barely been
tapped, and they want to change
that. A major component of their
strategy is the promotion and
advertising they do for their own
comic art studio. Because comic
art is read and loved by just
about everyone, these efforts have
brought no little attention to themselves and their work. Of one ad,
which appeared in a major illustration showcase, Schumer says,
"Before this ad ran, we were
doing 90 percent comp art and
storyboards. After it appeared,
the response and jobs it engen-
dered inverted that ratio to 90
percent finished illustration and
10 percent production art. Even
at a cost of seventy-five hundred
dollars, the ad paid for itself many
times over."

▲ *Three-dimensional mailer for Arlen Schumer and
Sherri Wolfgang's Dynamic Duo Studio*

▲ Schumer and Wolfgang's own wedding invitation

▲ Dynamic Duo ads are an important facet of the studio's promotion efforts, incorporate work done for clients

## ANNUAL MANUAL

*Schum & Stober, Inc.*
*McLean, Virginia*

In issuing a self-promotion that reveals their substantial knowledge about annual reports, advertising and marketing designers Schum & Stober positioned themselves as experts in the process. Created at a cost of about forty-five dollars per copy, the twenty-four page, full-color brochure was sent to key persons with annual report accountability for a targeted number of Fortune 500 corporations. In addition, the designers offered the piece "to anyone who requested it who could demonstrate their need for it." Intended to be both informative and entertaining, the book imparts valuable information and ideas to help make the annual report process a little less grueling. "We wanted the piece to be kept as both a reference piece and a working tool for use during present and future annual report seasons," says art director Guy Schum. "So far, it has landed us at least two major annual reports and several awards for design."

▲ Schum & Stober's self-promotion, "The Production of an Annual Report," is a
guide to project management for this premier corporate publication

## BRIGHT IDEAS

*Heller Breene*
*Boston, Massachusetts*

Promotions produced by Heller Breene for the S.D. Warren Company's line of coated printing papers do more than display the products' excellent reproducibility. They challenge the reader with witty concepts, clever copy, and dazzling special effects. The first of these, entitled "Garden Cameos," presents photomontage, hand-colored photography, unusual varnishing techniques, double gate-folds, and complete production notes for a promotion that is both informative and visually captivating; the second, called "Twins," features photography of just that—several sets of identical twins—reproduced in varying combinations. Designer Cheryl Heller reports that each of these pieces (which together numbered 400,000 copies) met with great success. The "Twins" piece, she says, "broke new ground in the variety and quantity of techniques achieved in a single piece," whereas the "Garden Cameos" brought "tremendous response from printers, designers, and production people."

▲ *"Twins" paper promotion, designed by Heller Breene for S.D. Warren*

# YOUNG, HOT, OVERWHELMINGLY FEMALE AGENCY SEEKS PASSIONATE WRITER FOR LATE NIGHTS AND LONG WEEKENDS. MUST BE ABLE TO HANDLE REJECTION.

Come on guys, show us what you're made of.
Call 617-737-6841 and ask for Chris Moody (Ms.).

## Heller Breene

▲ *Heller Breene's copywriter recruiting ad was aimed*

*at attracting a creative, hard-working male, brought numerous responses.*

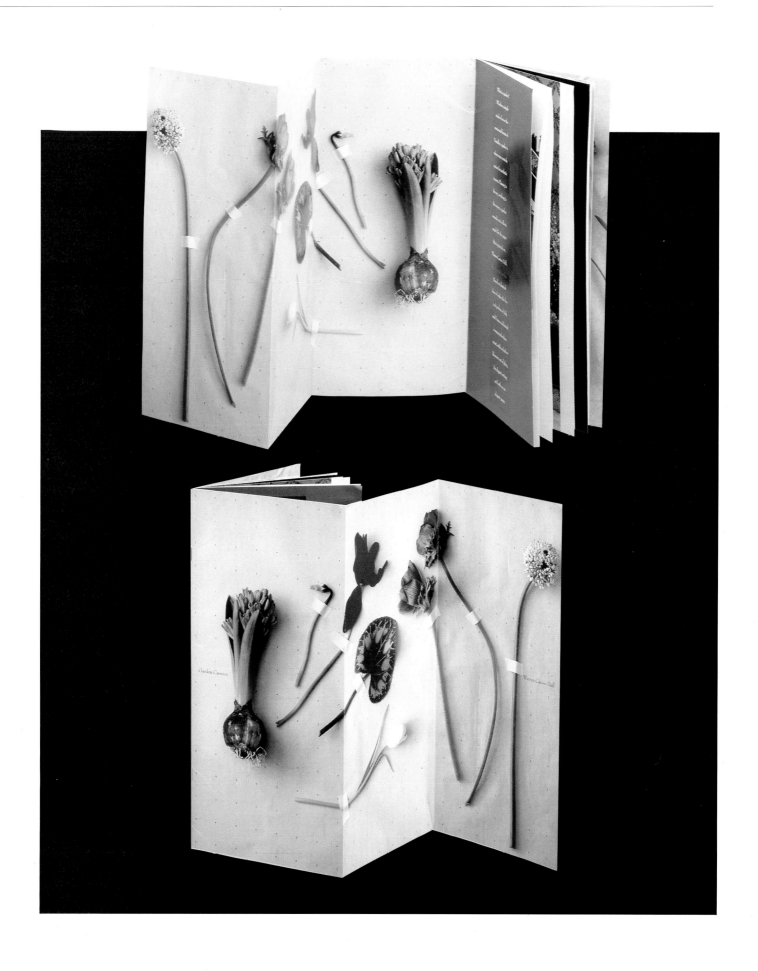

▲ Heller Breene's "Garden Cameos" paper promotion for S.D. Warren

## CRYSTAL INVENTION

*Chermayeff & Geismar
Associates
New York, New York*

What was conceived as a straightforward documentation of Chermayeff & Geismar Associates, trademarks work turned into an exercise in invention. In the search for an innovative cover, the designers hit upon a unique encapsulated liquid crystal film— a layer of liquid crystal (the same stuff used in pocket calculator readouts) trapped between layers of film and cover stock. The materials had never been used as the cover of a publication before, but C&GA gave it a try. Now in use for ten years, the covers themselves still amaze all who see them—or, more accurately, touch them: the laminate is heat sensitive and, like a "mood ring," changes color with changes in body temperature. Indeed, touch is a basic issue in the design firm's use of this book, which through the years has nearly doubled in size as new projects have been added. Rather than send it ahead or mail it cold (at about $150 per copy, the book is far too expensive for that), C&GA principals use the projects inside as a visual aid when making a presentation to a potential client. "When you're talking about print of any kind," says C&GA partner Steff Geissbuhler, "you want to touch the real thing. Slides of printed pieces have an unreality to them. Also, we put effort and pride into our supervision and execution; with slides, the texture of the stock and the feel of the piece doesn't come through."

▲ *Chermayeff & Geismar Associates' trademarks promotion is one inch thick and bound with a unique, interlocking double spiral. Cover is a heat-sensitive encapsulated liquid crystal film*

## ROCK, ROLL 'N' PROMO

*Manhattan Design*
*New York, New York*

Frank Olinsky and Pat Gorman, founders of Manhattan Design, are well known among rockers—they've designed album covers for the likes of Billy Idol and Duran Duran, as well as the well-known MTV logo. When they wanted to expand their client base beyond the R'n'R area, they elected to produce an oversized, black-and-white folder with a striking portrait of themselves on the cover. "We wanted to let people know we're not only New Wave rock-and-roll," Olinsky says. "So the piece had to be fairly sophisticated." About one thousand of the 17" x 24" (when open) mailers were sent in a sturdy board envelope to prospects in entertainment, sportswear design, and retail. The promotion not only generated new business in those areas but also was picked up by the design press for some spot publicity.

▲ *Manhattan Design's poster-sized mailer*

## CONCRETE EVIDENCE

*Concrete/The Office of*
*Jilly Simons*
*Chicago, Illinois*

Following the trend of Chicago graphic design studios, Jilly Simons chose a single, strong name when she opened her own firm—Concrete. Part of the task of announcing this name was the need to explain its derivation. Sent inside a minimally designed, more formal engraved announcement, a black-and-white postcard did the trick. "The card set the future tone of Concrete and its attitude," Simons explains. "Its design was a play of contrasts. The outside card was understated and tongue-in-cheek—similar to wedding invitations or law firm announcements. The insert played off concrete poetry and the visual capacity of words." Taking the metaphor further, Simons produced another promotion to celebrate her firm's first anniversary—the Concrete logo, carved into a miniature concrete block. Double-wrapped inside a mock telephone white page and a board overleaf, the block also served as a holiday greeting. "The block plays on the name of our 'hard-working' firm, and the wrapping is in the same vernacular," Simons says. "The positive response from both the design community and our target audience of friends, clients, and suppliers was overwhelming." Total cost of both promotions was fifteen hundred dollars.

▲ *Concrete logo-block celebrates the firm's first anniversary*

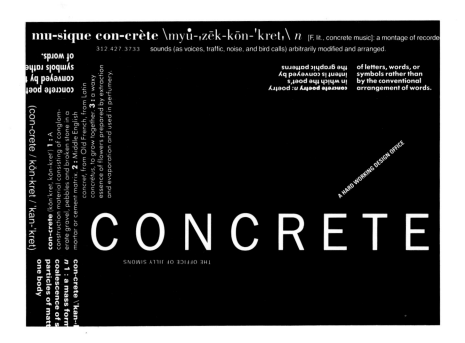

▲ *Concrete's opening announcement is an exercise in concrete poetry*

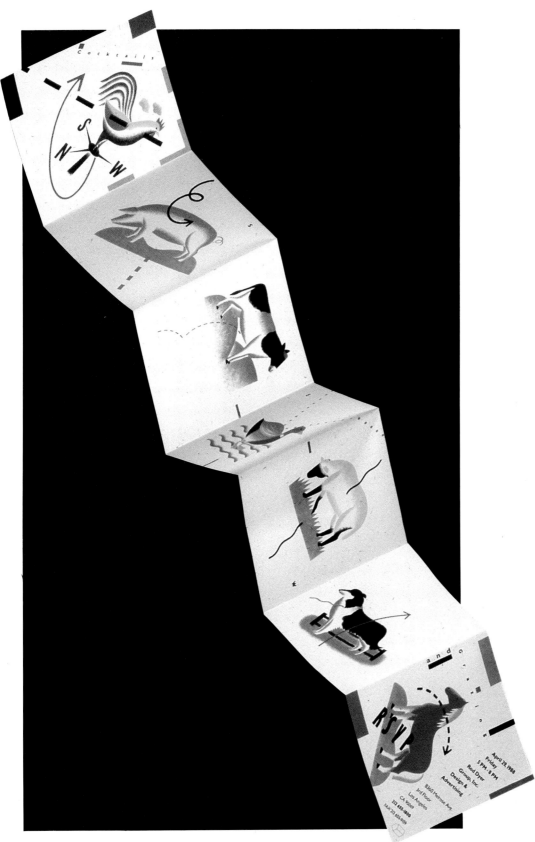

## SOMETHING TO CROW ABOUT

*Rod Dyer Group*
*Los Angeles, California*

For some time, the Rod Dyer Group has reached its entertainment-oriented clients with personal presentations and a kit of promotional folders that highlight the firm's successful projects in motion picture and theater advertising, restaurants and interiors, and packaging and business communications design. While the folders may not legitimately take full credit for the Group's success, they are part of a growth story that led, eventually, to new quarters—in a new, barn-shaped building with what Rod Dyer calls a "rural, wide-open atmosphere." To announce the move and celebrate its significance, group designer Steve Twigger created a mini-campaign with an upbeat, country theme. The focal point of each piece is a cocky weathervane; papers used are crafty and natural. While it's difficult to put a dollar value on moving/party promotions such as this, the entire campaign—postcard, Rolodex card, invitation, and T-shirt—received a lot of comment. And the party was a huge success.

▲ *The Rod Dyer Group's "rooster" moving materials suggest the new office's country atmosphere*

▲ *Promotional folders used to reach prospects by the Rod Dyer Group*

▲ New name, logo, and graphic identity for Waters Design Associates

reflects firm's commitment to "refreshing design for the inquisitive mind"

## FRESH WATERS

*Waters Design Associates*
*New York, New York*

A key element in John Waters's growth plan for his graphic design business is to shift some of the emphasis away from himself and onto the very capable designers on his staff. A first step in achieving this goal was to change the name of the studio, from John Waters Associates to the less personal Waters Design Associates. In developing an image for the new name, he made a conscious choice to play down the corporate design for which he is perhaps best known. Instead, he favored what he calls the fun aspects of the firm's other areas of expertise—marketing communications, environmental design, and electronic imaging. His new logo—a tongue-in-cheek $H_2Os$—express a key concern—that graphic design should be intelligent, refreshing, and invite viewer participation. Another facet of Waters's business has been to expand into computer imaging. As a pioneer in CAD for graphic communications, he has formed a separate company to produce, exhibit, and sell computer-generated artworks. A brochure, designed to accompany an exhibition of the studio's computer art prints allows each Waters designer to speak from his or her own experience of the latest technology. The "Visual Chemistry" exhibition brochure quickly snared two commissions—one from another design firm, and the second, a large environmental installation.

▲ *"Visual Chemistry" brochure accompanied exhibition of Waters Design Associates'*

*computer-generated artworks, is used to sell CAD for a variety of applications*

## Paper Promotions

Paper promotions from Waters Design Associates display the studio's more whimsical side. Designed, and in some cases illustrated, with a Lightspeed computer system, these small booklets stick close to budget and produce a lot of bang for the buck. Aimed at revitalizing existing lines and/or introducing line extensions, all have boosted paper sales. Particularly successful was the piece for Curtis Tuscan; orders for the new Tuscan Terra quickly outstripped the mill's ability to produce it.

▲ *Paper promotions for James River use a variety of techniques within an intimate scale*

## JOINT DIVIDENDS

*Fitch RichardsonSmith*
*Worthington, Ohio*

When RichardsonSmith, an Ohio-based firm, decided to accept a merger offer from the London-based Fitch & Company, they needed an announcement right away. With only one month until the official press conference publicizing the merger, the new, international organization had not even settled on a name. Nonetheless, the designers moved forward in producing a handsome, sepia-toned brochure that would explain to conference attendees the new entity's expanded capabilities. Produced at under one dollar per copy, the brochure not only did its job but won two graphic design awards and finds continued use with all press materials and information kits sent to prospective clients. Since the merger, additional materials have been created that support the new Fitch Richardson-Smith identity. One, a Christmas card, offers a toast with a real English tea bag (at under three dollars a cup, a "smashing" success); another, a cluster of postcards in a die-cut folder, cost three dollars each to position the company as experts in package design.

▲ *Brochure created to announce merger of RichardsonSmith with Fitch & Company*

▲ Holiday greeting from the newly formed Fitch RichardsonSmith is

embossed, illustrated, and includes a spot of tea

▲ Postcard packet promotes Fitch RichardsonSmith's expertise as package designers.
Each individual card highlights one successful project, utilizes pertinent buzzwords
("explains," "competes," "persuades," and so on) to characterize the concept

## GOING FISHING

*Anthony Russell, Inc.*
*New York, New York*

Anthony Russell believes there is no one way to get a prospective buyer's attention. So, promotion from his graphic design firm takes varied forms. The most important element, he thinks, is frequency, and his three major self-promotion efforts are all serial events. Perhaps most successful are his "quarterly reports" (actually issued three or four times per year). At a cost of three to four thousand dollars each issue, he sends about twelve hundred copies to prospective clients of all types. "Their bulletin flavor is more interesting than a definitive brochure," Russell says, "which is static and quickly outdated." While he adds that it's difficult to say exactly when these bulletins work, several projects have come in directly from their issue. A softer sell is a joint promotional magazine, called *U.S. Eye*, which he produces with Southeastern Printing and sends to design and photography buyers. Russell measures the success of this piece by three yardsticks: "Readers want to subscribe to it, photographers want to appear in it, and corporations want a corporate magazine just like it." But the softest sell of all takes place while adrift above the continental shelf—Russell's annual fishing party for clients and staff. Is it successful? "Very," says Russell. "In 1988, more than sixty people came. We drank a few beers and caught 350 fish."

▲ The bulletin flavor of Anthony Russell's quarterly reports keep clients and prospects abreast of what's new from Russell's design firm

▲ Annual fishing parties for clients and Anthony Russell staff allow for informal

contact and a little schmoozing—in addition to the invitation and free T-shirt

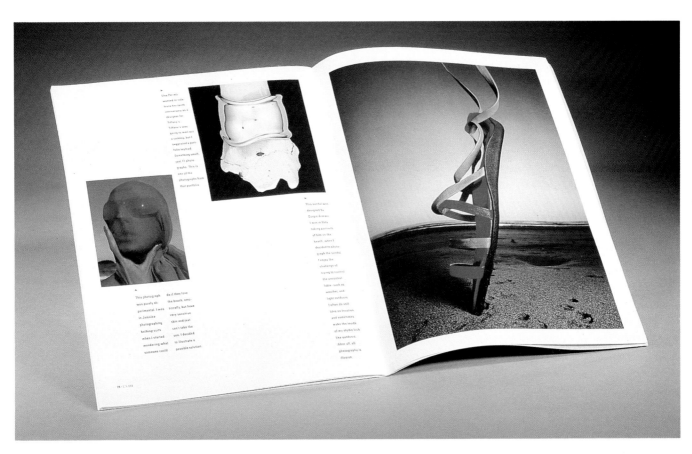

▲ A promotional photography magazine produced by Russell and Southeastern Printing

## A QUON-DARY OF PROMO

*Mike Quon Design Office*
*New York, New York*

Mike Quon makes no bones about it: his aggressive approach to promotion isn't loved—or even understood—by everyone. "I'm at times shameless in calling attention to myself," the designer/illustrator says. Indeed, Quon estimates that he spends as much time creating his promotional work as he does assignments. "It's a matter of survival," he adds. "If I stop, my business level may shift." With a staff of eight to support, Quon continually combs newspapers and magazines, looking for new agencies and art directors to add to his mailing list. Now running at around one thousand names, he uses these selectively—some promotions go to all, some to a few. "You have to have a certain sensitivity about whom to reach at what time," he observes with Confucian clarity. Nor has he been shy about using his ethnicity as a jumping off point: a Chinese-American, born in Hollywood, he has a sense of the theatrical and blends it especially well in his Q logo series, for which he photographs his Q logo-mark, in various forms, around the world. But as a man of many talents, Quon also creates mailers that focus on his signature illustration style or reveal the humorous edge to his design sensibilities. His casual bombardment of prospects from three to fifteen times a year has brought him editorial exposure, merchandising offers, and countless design and illustration assignments.

▲ *Perhaps best known of Mike Quon's promotions is his ten-year-old Q logo campaign, aimed at getting his name and logo wide exposure*

▲ Quon's fortune-cookie moving announcement doubles as a Chinese New Year's greeting

▲ After working with an art director, Quon creates a personal "thank you" with
an ink drawing and press-on color. He estimates that he spends three hundred dollars per year
in time and materials (primarily frames) creating these pieces, and that five hundred of them hang in New York City alone

## QUALITY IMPRESSION

*The Office of
Michael Manwaring
San Francisco, California*

After fifty years of providing fine printing to businesses in the San Francisco Bay area, Warren's Waller Press wanted a promotion piece that would impress potential clients with the firm's quality and capabilities. Rather than produce a brochure full of glossy four-color photography, designer Michael Manwaring created a complex, production-oriented promotion with graphic illustrations to highlight the printer's philosophical underpinnings. Some ten thousand of the twelve-page brochures were printed for use as send-aheads and leave-behinds. "We make cold calls on people who don't know us," ways Waller sales rep, Freddy Hahne. "It's fine to send samples, but this is verbal capabilities. And, when a potential client receives something fancy in the mail, it makes the followup call that much easier." As an added bonus, Hahne says, the book has facilitated marketing efforts to more sophisticated print buyers who want visual proof of a printer's abilities with more advanced reproduction techniques.

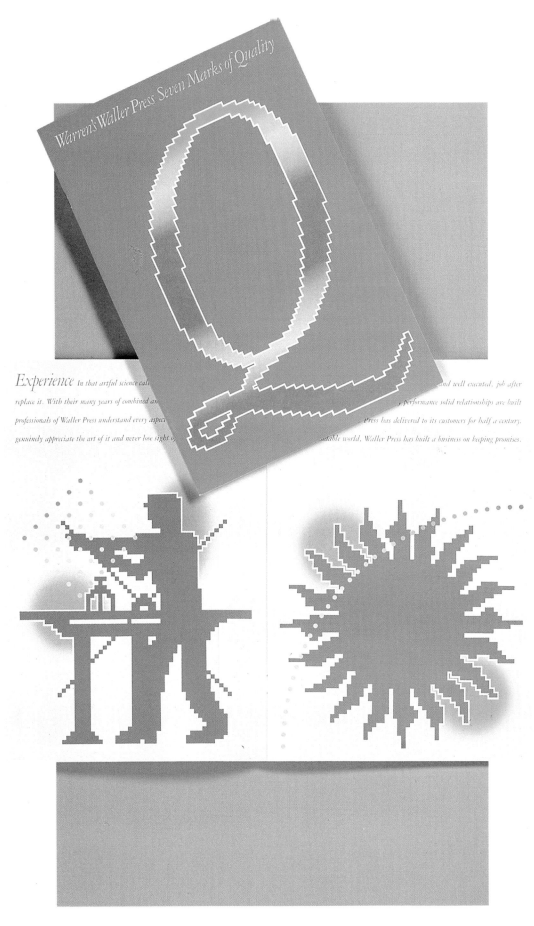

▲ *Michael Manwaring's brochure for Warren's Waller Press
is a valuable tool for Waller's thirteen sales reps*

▲ *Gerald Reis's posters for Mitsumura Printing, Japan*

## ORIENTAL INFLUENCES

*Gerald Reis & Company
San Francisco, California*

After his work appeared in a book about five American and two Japanese graphic designers, Gerald Reis was asked by the book's printers, Mitsumura Printing, to produce four posters to promote the printing house in Japan. Given free rein, Reis took the opportunity to create some images that had been in his mind for some time and that would serve several purposes. One poster—a free-form figure "/" that suggests the title of the book—was conceived as a promotion for the book itself, *Seven,* published by Graphic-sha. Another—a stylized drawing of a plate of figs—was created as a "thank you" to a client. The remaining two were more or less pure promotions for his own firm, one expressing his love of opera and Japanese imagery (a painting of Madame Butterfly) and one reflecting the various disciplines his staff has to offer. While most of the posters were distributed in Japan, Reis used his much smaller allotment as gifts, prints for sale, and framed art in his own studio. In this last context, he says, they have received the most attention, simply by making visiting clients aware of the broad scope of his studio's services.

## DRAWING BUSINESS

*Alan E. Cober*
*Ossining, New York*

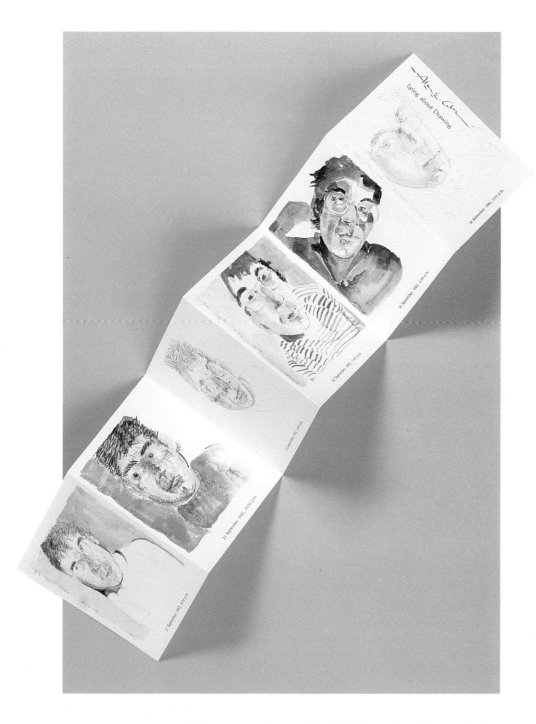

▲ *Cober generally includes the lighter side of his work when answering a portfolio request. His "Lying About Drawing," which he made from a sickbed, is an apt example*

After years of representation by one of New York's top agents, illustrator Alan Cober left the stable to pursue a maverick course of self-promotion. Reckoning that, while his editorial work had gained him wide recognition, not so many knew of his corporate assignments, he embarked on a strategic campaign aimed at buyers of art for corporate publications. With the headline "Corporate Cober," which was coined with the help of art director Kent Dicken, Cober's campaign made its debut against the gray flannel cover of a mailer announcing his talk before the Art Directors Club of Indiana. By negotiating an overrun of the announcement for use as a general promotion, Cober also hit upon an effective way to publicize his corporate and social commentary illustration. He expanded the campaign by placing carefully conceived ads in various talent directories, under the same headline. The strategy worked: Each ad and mailer brought many requests for portfolios, which he filled with tearsheets from his twenty years of corporate illustration and personal visual commentary. Assignments got bigger and better—so much so that Cober estimates his income has more than doubled since the campaign began.

▲ Illustrator Alan Cober's primary campaign, "Corporate Cober," aims at making buyers aware of his sizable but little-known work for corporate publications

▲ An announcement for a talk before the Connecticut Art Directors Club utilizes illustrations originally executed around a "dollar bill" theme for the American Society for Quality Control. Cober used a large overrun as a self-promotional mailer

## MILESTONES

*Summerford Design
Dallas, Texas*

A documentation and a celebration, Summerford Design's capabilities book is organized around Jack Summerford's first twenty years in the graphic design business. Sensitively written and edited, the tale begins with the designer's graduation from Washington University (St. Louis) and traces his career, through noteworthy design projects, up until and beyond his opening of his own graphic design office. Not counting design time, Summerford reckons he spent at least thirty-five thousand dollars to produce the fifty-two-page, full-color, perfect-bound book. The promotion was sent to both existing and potential clients, as well as certain professional colleagues, "to generate and solidify business," Summerford says, "and also to cut down on the number of samples" he'd been sending out. While the success of the book, he says, is difficult to measure, he feels it has "worked well in all areas." And work it must—Summerford has no plans to update the book until the next milestone—his thirty-year mark.

▲ *Summerford Design's capabilities book celebrates graphic designer Jack Summerford's first twenty years in the business. Designed and written by Summerford, it's an example of his belief in keeping his firm small. "When you buy Summerford Design," he writes, "you get Summerford design"*

▲ *Summerford's stationery is redesigned every time a current issue runs out*

▲ *Christmas cards from R.L. Meyer Advertising
are designed around changing themes.*

## MADE TO ORDER

*R.L. Meyer Advertising
Milwaukee, Wisconsin*

To reach prospective clients, R.L. Meyer Advertising creates individual, handmade promotion pieces conceptualized to land an account. For openers, the client receives a handcarved "talking stick"—an embellished variation of the traditional, native American stick used to signify a speaker's turn in tribal meetings. The Meyer talking stick tells prospects that the agency is ready to listen to the client's advertising needs—and also provides the prospect with an interesting conversation piece. After a Meyer team has met with the prospect and made a proposal, a second, more personalized promotion is sent. This one-of-a-kind piece is constructed by a staff member for the cost of materials and always includes some kind of visual/verbal joke. A promotion aimed at a manufacturer of bathroom fixtures, for example, consisted of two of the manufacturer's faucets and the copy line, "For your next hot project, tap our resources." A promotion for a soft drink company used crumpled soda cans and the tag, "We'll give you a Jolly Good way to flatten the competition." These promotions, says copywriter Effie Meyer, both demonstrate the agency's eagerness and creativity and show clients that they are special to the agency. And, while the pieces have won awards, more important is the good will they have generated among prospects.

# We'll give you a Jolly Good way...

# To flatten the competition.

R.L. Meyer Advertising

▲ For a soft drink manufacturer

*Some of the personalized, one-of-a-kind promotions that R.L. Meyer Advertising has used to land accounts*

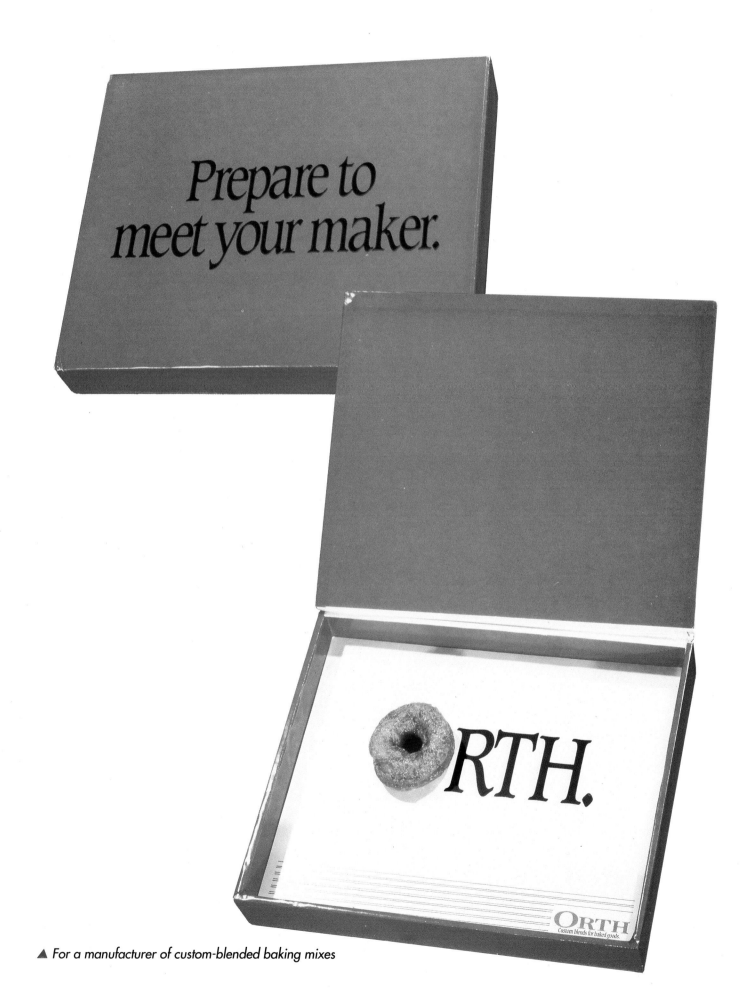

▲ *For a manufacturer of custom-blended baking mixes*

## PROLIFIC PROMOS

*Steven Guarnaccia*
*New York, New York*

Illustrator Steven Guarnaccia loves to draw. Indeed, he says he leaves few surfaces undrawn upon and has even irked one of his best clients by absently doodling on the art director's blotter. Guarnaccia also finds it very difficult to make decisions about his own promotion design, and he's discovered that, by keeping all of his random doodles, he has amassed a sizable store of potential promotions. Guarnaccia mails out at least two promotions a year, if only to keep his latest work before his clients' eyes; these might be a holiday greeting, a special announcement, or something sent for the fun of it. "I love getting stuff in the mail," he says, "and I just want to join the circle of mail art." When the need—or the mood—arises, Guarnaccia digs through his store. Often an image will spark an idea; in any case, he says, his own images are like found art and allow him the relaxation of art directing—rather than drawing on demand. Produced more or less off-the-cuff, the ebullient promotions serve to display to potential clients new directions, to remind old clients that he's there, and to get his phone ringing again.

▲ *Guarnaccia's self-portrait mask promotion evokes a*

*character from the Comedia del'Arte*

▲ *Postcard announcing*

*exhibitions of*

*Guarnaccia's work*

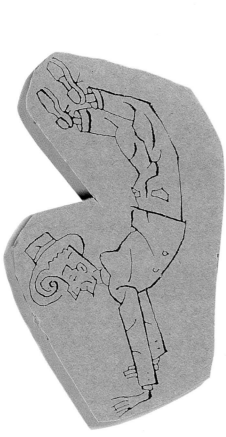
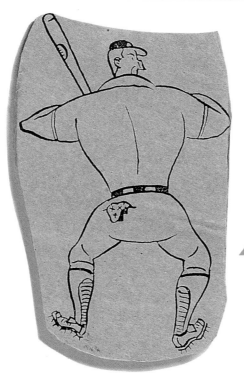

▲ New Year's greetings were copied
onto kraft paper, then glued
to corrugated cardboard
and cut to random shapes

▲ Guarnaccia's business card

▲ Birth announcement for
Guarnaccia's son Jasper.
Co-art director/designer:
Susan Hochbaum

## YULE BOOKS

*Samata Associates*
*Dundee, Illinois*

For graphic designers Pat and Greg Samata, the Christmas holidays offer a rare opportunity to acknowledge the contribution made by their employees all year long. The medium is a Samata Associates Christmas greeting that both pictures staff members and allows them to share their own family recipes and traditions. The one departure from this rule was a 1988 greeting to clients and friends that stemmed from a studio project—to promote and design Chicago's Museum of Science and Industry's annual masque ball. These somewhat elaborately produced books, says Pat Samata, get more and more difficult to top each year, both in design and subject matter. Still, the firm plans to continue its efforts. "The books are a great morale-booster for the people behind the scenes here," says Pat. "It's not often that they get credited for their work."

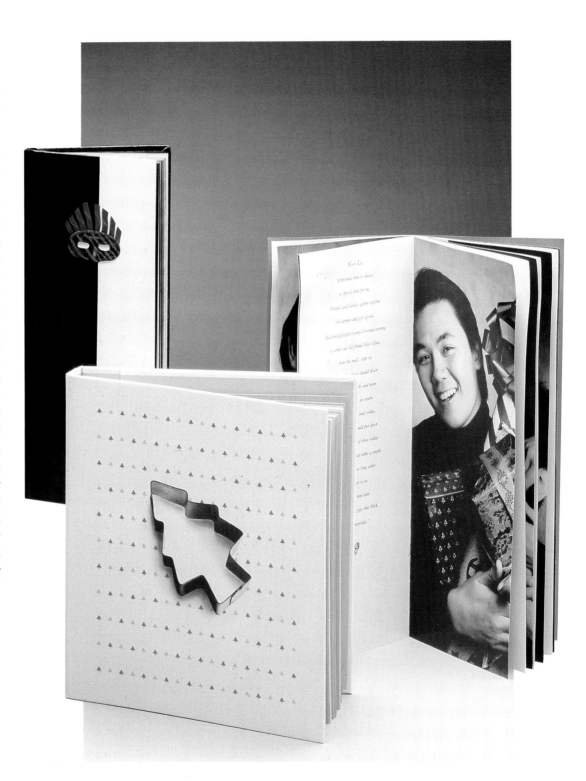

▲ Christmas greetings from Samata Associates are expressions of thanks both to clients and to employees. Here, Samata staff can share holiday memories and family recipes, or simply celebrate the coming of the New Year

## THINK INK

*The Ink Tank*
*New York, New York*

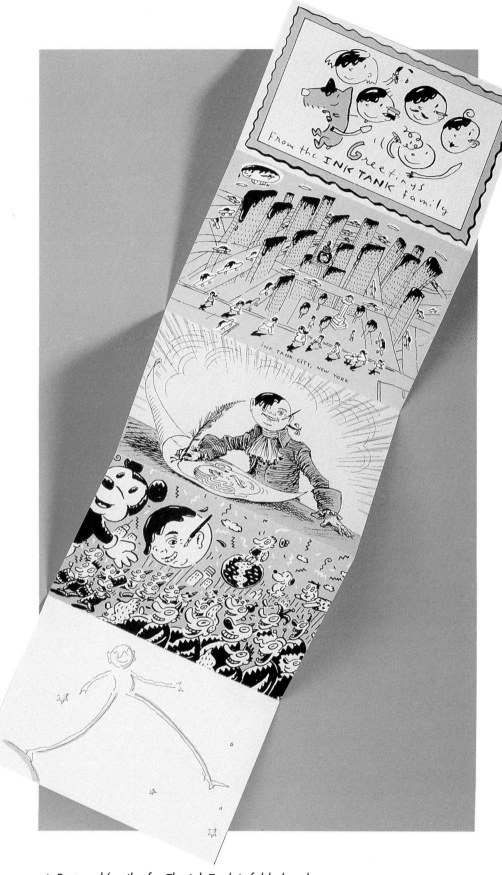

"Like any studio," says R.O. Blechman, "we want our promotion to be the kind that's referred to often." For this reason, Blechman's Ink Tank animation parlor in New York issues a yearly postcard series that features the work of several animators and is small enough to be easily stored. "Things like posters take up too much space," Blechman opines, "and in the end will be thrown away. Our postcards are fresh, usable, and storable. They're more like receiving a gift than a promotion." And, at a cost of six hundred to eight hundred dollars for two thousand sets of five postcards, he adds, they're economical enough to hand out on any occasion. Recipients include current and past clients and prospects already considering Ink Tank for a commission. Bolstering this mailing are a space ad run twice yearly in *Adweek*—a stratagem that has brought as many as six calls in one day—and the occasional announcement for one of Blechman's speaking engagements. The one thing that all of Ink Tank's promotions have in common, however, is a sense of humor. "Animation studios usually show stills in a grid format," Blechman says. "We want to present our work in a fresh context, without a hard sell."

▲ Postcard/mailer for The Ink Tank is folded and

sent in an envelope to current and past clients

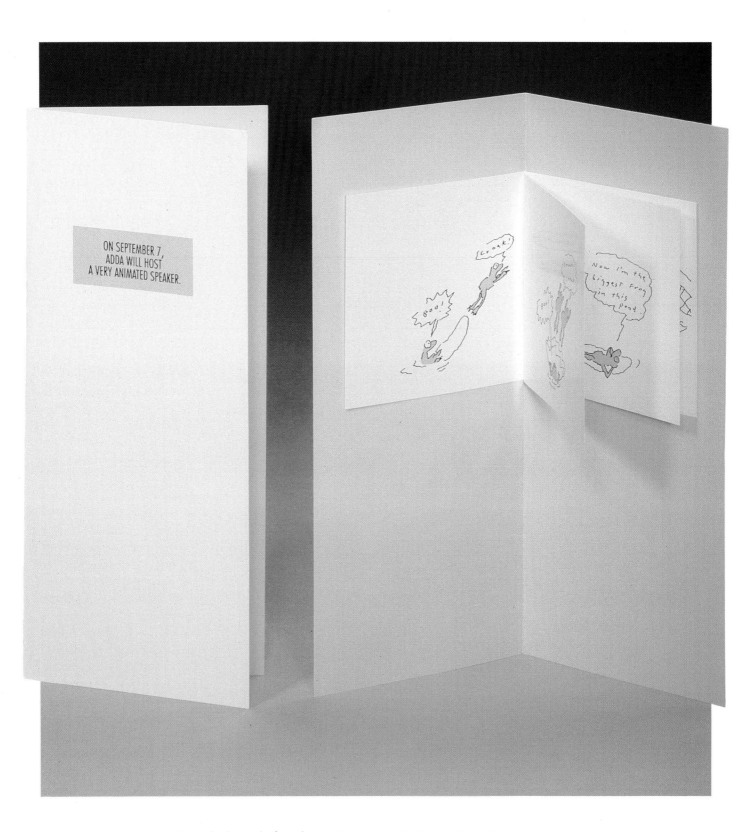

▲ *Invitation to a talk by R.O. Blechman before the Art Directors & Designers Association*

*of New Orleans. Sequential drawings in interior mini-booklet conclude,*

*"It is better to be a small fry in a big pond than a big fry in a small pan."*

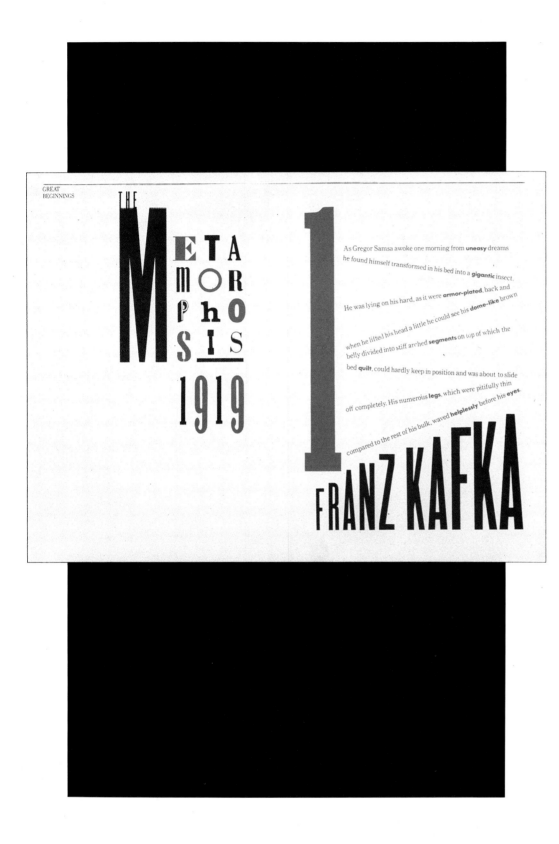

GREAT
BEGINNINGS

THE METAMORPHOSIS 1919

As Gregor Samsa awoke one morning from **uneasy** dreams he found himself transformed in his bed into a **gigantic** insect. He was lying on his hard, as it were **armor-plated**, back and when he lifted his head a little he could see his **dome-like** brown belly divided into stiff arched **segments** on top of which the bed **quilt** could hardly keep in position and was about to slide off completely. His numerous **legs**, which were pitifully thin compared to the rest of his bulk, waved **helplessly** before his **eyes**.

FRANZ KAFKA

▲ *Koppel & Scher's "Great Beginnings" partnership*

*announcement emphasizes the partners' talent for type styling*

*Koppel & Scher*
*New York, New York*

Promotion from Terry Koppel and Paula Scher's design office reflects the designers' typographic talents as well as their considerable wit. Since the mailings are each created to convey a specific bit of information—a new address, a party, a speaking engagement—the partners can focus less on marketing strategy and more on enjoying themselves with the project. "We don't promote ourselves through our promotion pieces," cautions Scher. "We do that through awards annuals, speaking engagements, and writing. These are what really maintain our visibility. When we do design a promotion, it's usually something for fun." But, as so often happens when people enjoy their work, the product here is especially memorable. The promotion sent at the inception of their partnership, for example, numbered their own union as one of several "Great Beginnings" and presented the opening paragraphs of famous novels, each designed in the graphic style of its own period. In typical self-deprecatory fashion, a moving announcement starts with the headline, "There goes the neighborhood," and the invitation to that office's office-warming welcomes guests to "stain [Koppel & Scher's] new carpets and burn their linoleum." "Our promotions are based on our personality", says Scher unabashedly, "and *we* don't like to take ourselves too seriously."

▲ Office-warming invitation is printed on a slice of linoleum

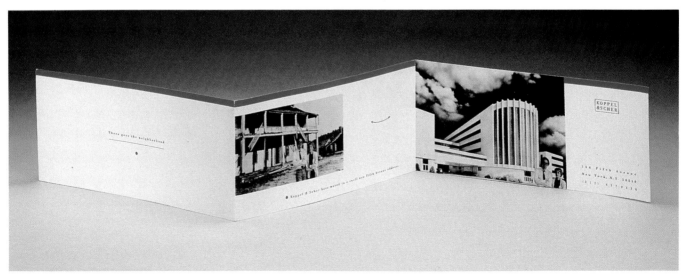

▲ Koppel & Scher announce their move to "a swell new Fifth Avenue address" with the warning, "There goes the neighborhood"

## Champion Paper Promotions

Koppel & Scher's promotions for Champion International's "Linen" printing paper incorporate the designers' love of typography and typographic embellishment. Designed with the understanding that no one promotion will be loved by every designer and paper specifier that receives it, the series seeks to create a stylish yet useful reference that won't soon be thrown away. "We thought that if we gave people a tool," Scher says, "even if they didn't like the way it looks, they'd keep it." By working off the old typefaces and dingbats that Koppel & Scher use all the time, the promotions have proved as good as Scher's word. "People use these books all the time," she says. "I still get comments about how well organized they are. Designers appreciate having all of these things in one place." Moreover, the client has their paper available in a handy reference marketwide. "It's been phenomenally successful," Scher adds. "We printed forty thousand, and they're totally gone."

▲ *Promotion series for Champion International makes use of Koppel & Scher's love of typographic embellishment as well as providing a "keeper" reference tool*

## CHOICE LAUNCH

*Fallon McElligott*
*Minneapolis, Minnesota*

When Weyerhauser Paper Company was ready to introduce its first new business paper in years, they called in ad agency Fallon McElligott to provide advertising and collateral support. "Historically speaking, Weyerhauser had a low profile in this segment, because most of our products were sold under private labels," explains Fred Dempsey, Weyerhauser's manager of advertising and sales promotion. "We needed to establish Weyerhauser as a significant factor in the office papers business." Called "First Choice," the new paper was specially created for use with state-of-the-art office technology—desktop publishing, laser and ink-jet printers, high-resolution copiers. Working with graphic designers McCool & Company, who produced the collateral, Fallon McElligott masterminded a print campaign that includes ads and inserts, teasers, mailers, and a handsome capabilities and sample pack. "Our aim was to create awareness of `First Choice' as a top-notch business paper," Says Tom Wilson, Fallon McElligott's account supervisor on the project, "and to bring `First Choice' to the front of people's minds when they're ordering paper." The campaign appears to have met its goals. "`First Choice' has been well received by our merchants," Dempsey says, "the vast majority of whom have put in substantial inventories of the product."

▲ *Direct-mail pieces, sent by paper merchants to office supply stores and printers, include a business reply card for a sample package of "First Choice"*

▲ Sample pack of "First Choice for Important Documents" includes business communications that
have been laser printed, ink-jet printed, xerographed, color-laser imaged, and lithographed on "First Choice"—
as well as a quantity of the paper sufficient to allow recipients to try it on their own office machines

## EVOLUTIONS

*Hornall Anderson
Design Works
Seattle, Washington*

The new graphic identity for Hornall Anderson Design Works was built on previous renditions of the same, particularly the "constructed" letterforms designed by Jack Anderson before he became partner to John Hornall. "Although we design for print, we've always had a certain sympathy toward architecture and three-dimensional work," Anderson says. "Our newest logotype conveys our understanding of how things are put together—not just what they look like." The interlocking monogram also expresses a sensitive marriage of the organic with the technological—a feeling that isn't lost on the design firm's clients. Finding expression, as it does, on business papers, employee materials, T-shirts, and architectural signing, the new look has brought a team spirit to Hornall Anderson's two dozen employees, and, because of its natural evolution, has made constructed letterforms something of a trademark for the firm.

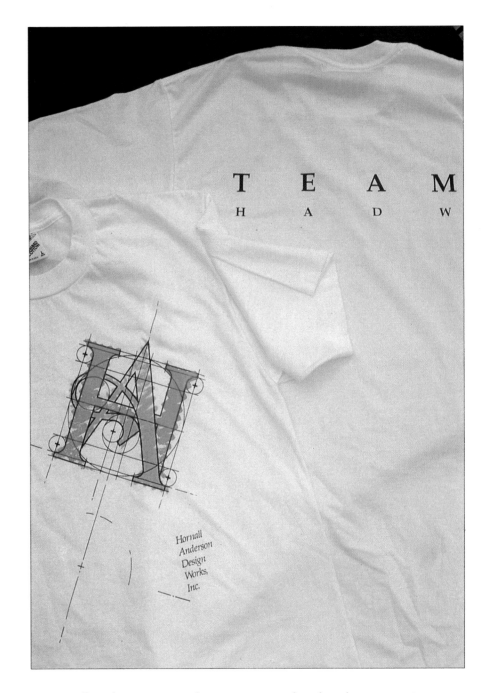

▲ *Hornall Anderson's newest logotype is reproduced on the company's T-shirt, as well as on business papers and architectural signing*

▲ *Print Northwest's selection of* N *letterforms*

## Print Northwest

Hornall Anderson Design Works' graphic identity for Print Northwest retains the strong, punchy flavor of the Seattle printer's previous identity in a fresher, more flexible mode. The system's basic device is a square form, "cocked to the northwest" (as art director Jack Anderson puts it) and fitted with one of eight *N* letterforms. By its chameleon-like effect, the program graphically conveys the printer's diverse capabilities and services, as well as the creative opportunities inherent in the print medium itself.

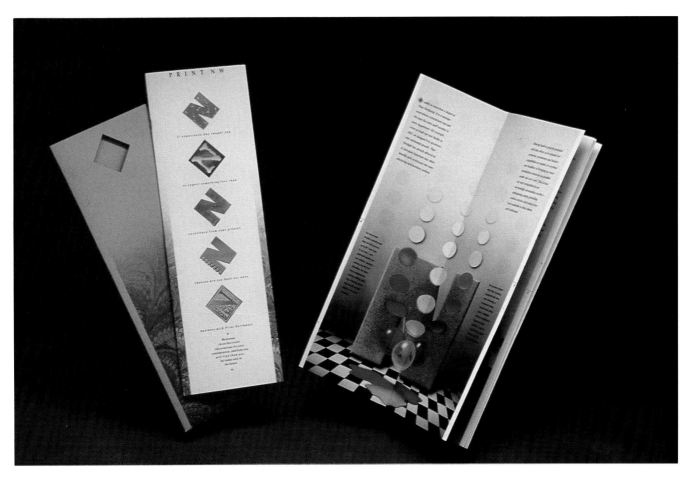

▲ *Print Northwest capabilities brochure*

## Neenah Paper Promotion

Hornall Anderson's promotion for Neenah Paper dispels some myths about the Pacific Northwest—that it's constantly raining, for example, or that the population is largely composed of salmon-eating, parka-wearing lumberjacks. Speaking to designers across the United States, the promotion displays Neenah Paper's versatility and, at the same time, comments on the homogeneous character of the American society.

## TRUTH AND SEQUENCES

*Jeff Moores*
*Honeoye, New York*

Jeff Moores's first flipbook was produced as an animation assignment while the illustrator was attending New York's Parsons School of Design. However, its subject matter—the trials and tribulations of commuting to New York City from across the Hudson River in New Jersey—as well as the idea of sequential, storytelling imagery was to remain with Moores long into professional life. "I spent so much time commuting that I either had to get angry and frustrated, or humor myself." Choosing the latter course, Moores vented his emotion in a series of serial promotions, beginning with a mailing of one thousand of the subway booklets. Later efforts brought other sequentials of commuters and beachgoers and "stills" of traffic jams and subway riders. At a cost of sixty cents to just over one dollar per copy, these engaging promotions have been amazingly effective, bringing jobs from *New York, Forbes* and *Golf* magazines, Whittle Communications, and a major promotion for Burger King. Nor has Moores's decision to leave the commuter's rat race for the wilds of western New York state caused a loss of interest on the part of his clients. Rather, the illustrator expects the theme of his promotions to change. "I've been working on several series involving living with nature," he says, "including shoveling the driveway here in the `Snow Belt.'"

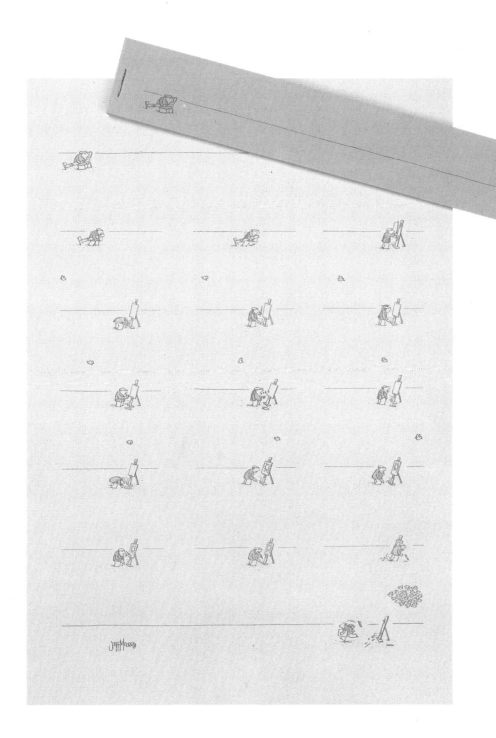

▲ *"Man vs. Bird"*

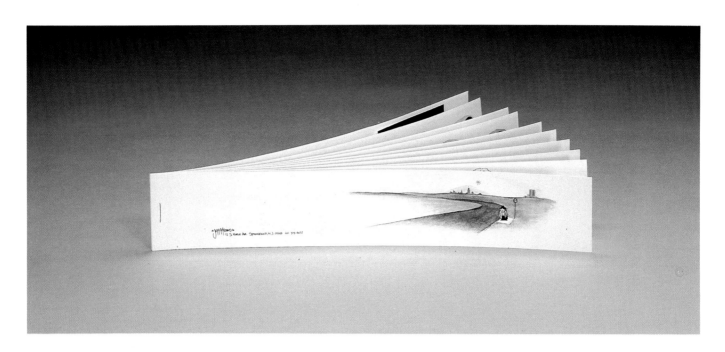

▲ The "Subway" flipbook that started Jeff Moores's sequential fascination and
brought him numerous jobs, including an eleven-page, forty-five-spot sequential for New York magazine

▲ Moores's promotional flier

▲ *Jeff Moores's commuter Christmas card*

## FAST TAKES

*Mike Salisbury
Communications
Torrance, California*

Graphic designer Mike Salisbury estimates that his firm sends close to two dozen self-promotion pieces each year, aimed largely at his movie-industry clients in Southern California. Such constant reminders are essential, he thinks, in this highly competitive business. "People don't always get the proper credit in the movie industry," Salisbury observes, "especially when an idea is used but executed by others." Salisbury's core promotion aims at correcting this kind of oversight by pointing out the significant movie advertising campaigns conceived and/or created by his firm. Produced in two colors by a speedy printer, the postcard mailers measure 11" x 4¹/₄" and cost around six hundred dollars for five hundred copies. Other occasional promotions and announcements, at slightly higher costs, may support this two-color series. "These promotions are all quick and easy to produce," Salisbury says, "and they get noticed."

# OSCARS?

Last year Mike Salisbury Communications created the concept for the **Moonstruck** advertising campaign. This year our idea was used for **Working Girl.** Two in a row? With over 200 movies behind us the odds seem pretty good. **Mike Salisbury Communications (213) 320-7660**

# The Most Pop Art.

An Adweek survey has chosen the Camel advertising as one of the year's most popular ad campaigns.
Thanks to Bob Cole and Barry Schweig of McCann-Erickson for letting Mike Salisbury Communications produce all the work. **Mike Salisbury Communications (213) 320-7660**

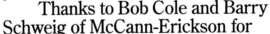

# Mikentosh

Mike Salisbury Communications has been joined by Alex Melli. A computer aided designer. He's the Apple of our eye. **Mike Salisbury Communications (213) 320-7660**

▲ *Mike Salisbury Communications' postcard mailers rely on catchy copy and*

*prominent use of company logo in an inexpensive, two-color format*

▲ Announcement of new company logo takes production cue from two-color series

▲ 1989 Calendar-postcard from Mike Salisbury Communications

## AMERICAN CLASSIC

*Cross Associates*
*Los Angeles, California*

Whether produced for themselves or for clients, promotions from Cross Associates exhibit a standard of taste and innovation that has made the design firm one of the best known, both in its West Coast home and across the United States. The firm's major effort is a handsome, square book that features Cross's classic solutions to a range of design problems. Now in its second edition, the new version has been updated with a bright color palette chosen to reposition the firm in a more "punchy, upbeat" manner. Used as a send-ahead and leave-behind, the book has been especially helpful in creating a positive image among the firm's corporate prospects. "The number of projects shown and their sense of presence have a cumulative effect," says principal James Cross. "In addition, the book's size, weight, and color, and the way it explains how we document the work we do—all of this creates a feeling of who we are." Cross estimates the five thousand copies of his "Red Book" would have cost his firm fifty to seventy thousand dollars to produce, had not most production services been traded out or donated.

Cross Associates                    Designers

▲ Poster announcing Cross Associates' new office in San Francisco

was the winner in an employee contest to create a single,

poetic statement about the process of design

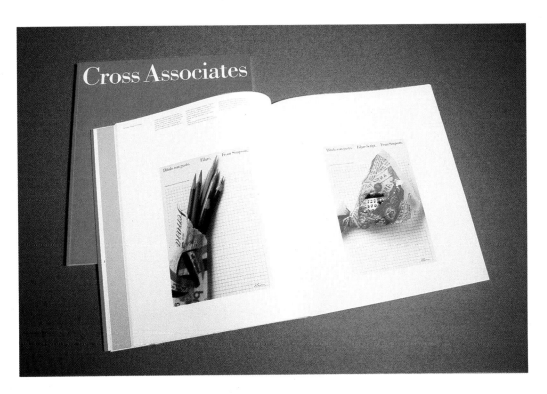

▲ Cross Associates' "Red Book" self-promotion is a great image-builder

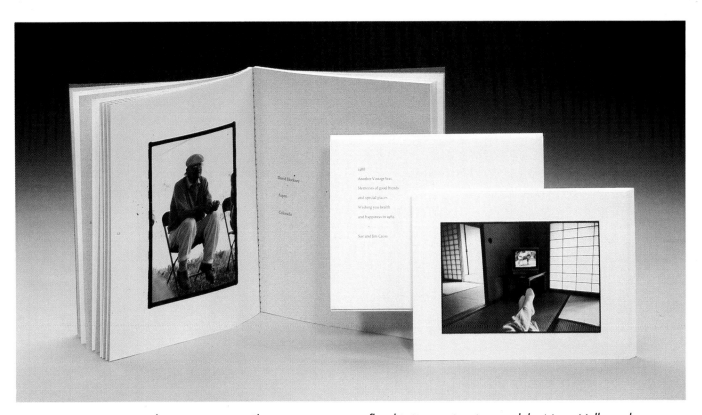

▲ James Cross's personal "Vintage Year" Christmas greetings reflect his interest in wines and the Napa Valley, where
he met his wife, Sue. The booklets allow the couple to celebrate their life and travels with close friends and associates

## Simpson Paper Promotions

Cross Associates serves as primary design consultants to Simpson Paper Company, and, says James Cross, is probably working on fifteen to twenty projects for the client at any one time. Through the last decade or so, this relationship has produced dozens of promotions that have resulted in impressive increases in sales of Simpson products. "Simpson's strategy," Cross notes, "is to put out a lot of small pieces, as opposed to a few big promotions, each year. The idea is to build on repetition, to be a continual presence through ads, mailers, samples, and creative promotions." While Simpson budgets are modest but adequate, he adds, part of his job is to watch money and scheduling and manage the many people and suppliers responsible for getting these numerous promotions out at the right time.

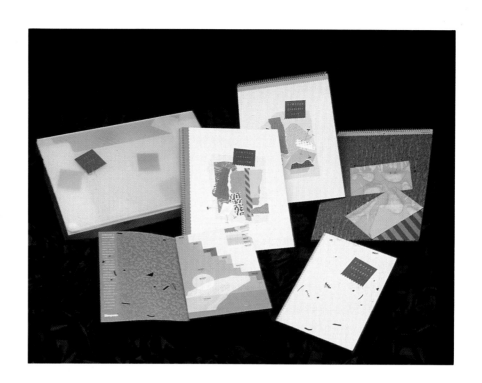

▲ An ambitious promotion for Simpson's Sundance papers puts coordinated swatchbooks and die-cut and illustrated promotions into their own plastic portfolio

▲ Die-cut, foil-stamped, and lithographed in six colors, Cross promotion for Simpson's Filare papers illustrates the impact that can be achieved with a less expensive sheet

▲ *Simpson Kashmir promotion captures the spirit and mystery*

*of that Himalayan stronghold through stunning photography and fine detail*

▲ *Cross Associates' Simpson Teton promotion featuring*

*Japanese art and design reflects the paper company's international scope*

## LOW PROFILE

*Crosby Associates, Inc.*
*Chicago, Illinois*

Graphic designer Bart Crosby has never been all that comfortable with the idea of aggressively promoting his design firm. "Our profile is serious and corporate," he says. "I don't want to do random, 'drop-in-the-box' mailings to let people know we're here. We're just not after that type of client." Instead, Crosby Associates uses the holiday season as the one opportunity to break from the corporate mold and reveal the firm's range of talent. "I generally assign our company greeting to one of the designers here, and let him or her run with it," Crosby says. "The only limitation is the budget, which is basically our outside costs." These holiday cards often have a labor-intensive aspect—like the torn cover that invited recipients to "tear into the new year," or a hand-folded greeting made from Japanese rice paper. The one time Crosby Associates *did* create a self-promotion, they did it subtly and elegantly, with flowers: three successive arrangements were sent to a select group of clients (as a thank-you) and prospects (as an introduction). Each black ceramic vase was hung with a simple tag identifying it within the series and bearing the corporate signature. While this promotion was more costly than the Christmas cards (which are printed at cost), it served to position Crosby Associates as uniquely creative designers.

▲ *The firm's one true self-promotion was said with flowers—three arrangements, sent serially, to selected clients and prospects.*

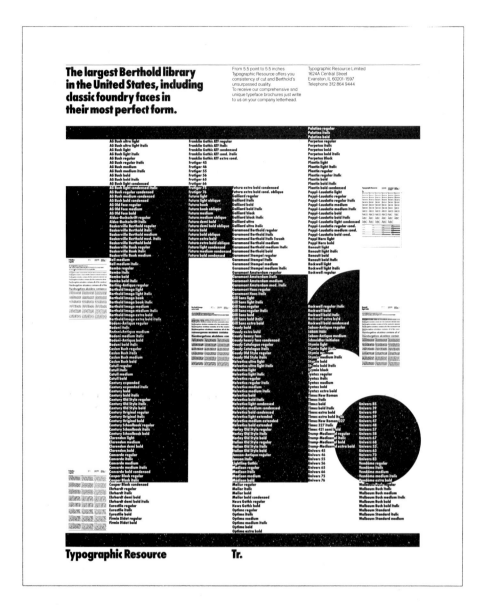

▲ *Ad appearing in* U&lc *magazine highlights*

*Typographic Resource's extensive Berthold library*

## Typographic Resource

Typographic Resource began as a cottage industry in a Chicago suburb. With the help of graphic designers Crosby Associates, the typographer moved to downtown Evanston and assumed a national presence. "They had typefaces no one else in the country had," says designer Bart Crosby, "including the largest collection of Berthold type in the United States." To meet the challenges of the larger market, Crosby developed the firm's name and an identity program based on a classic typographic rendering of its initials, *Tr*. Since his client, Harvey Hunt, is a real typographer, Crosby says, it was easy to bring the various components of the system on line—including a handsome tabloid-style newsletter roughed by Crosby and executed by Hunt on Tr.'s own CAD system. The venture—and the promotion—has been so successful that Typographic Resource will soon be offering its state-of-the-art CAD capabilities to all of its customers, too.

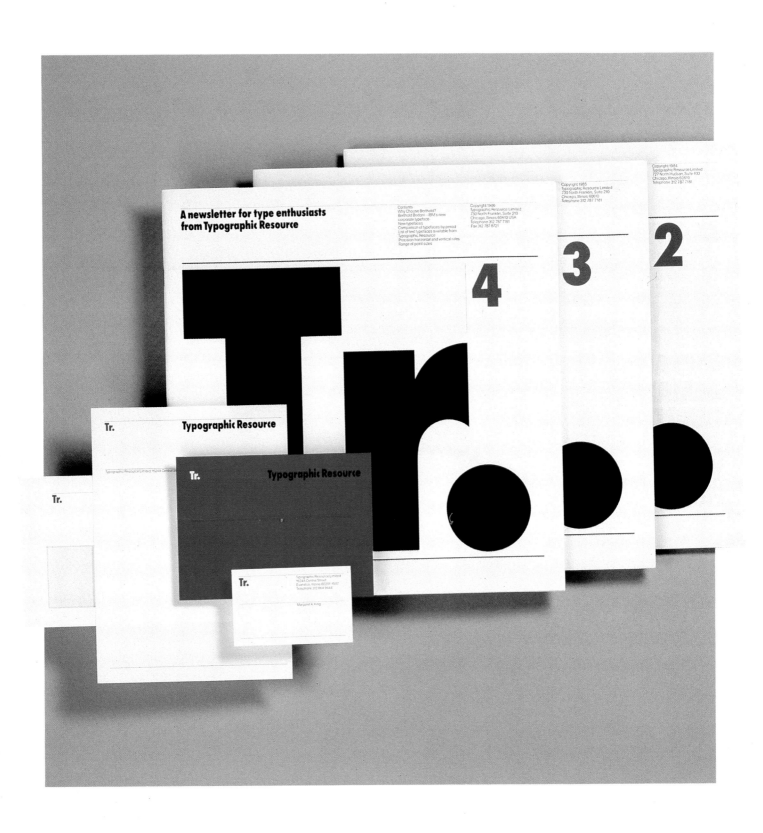

▲ Starting with the company name, designers Crosby Associates created a complete communications

package for Typographic Resource. Typographic Resource's newsletter contains historical aspects of

Berthold typography as well as news about the typographer's products and services

## A PASSION FOR PROMO

*Javier Romero*
*Design/Illustration*
*New York, New York*

Javier Romero specializes in what he calls "impact graphics"—contemporary graphic design and illustration for one-time, special applications. His self-promotions fit into this category, too, and like his work for corporations, advertising agencies, and publishing houses, they are eye-catching, exciting, and colorful. Romero's bedrock promotions—ads placed in talent directories—may be compendiums of his commissioned work, but in the four or more mailings he does each year, anything goes. He estimates he spends twenty-five thousand to thirty thousand dollars a year keeping his name—and work—in front of his market. "The field is too competitive," he says. "No matter how good you are, you have to let people know you're there and doing things. I have a real commitment to paying attention to my promotion—I just couldn't do without it." The awareness Romero has built over the years seems to have paid off. "I get a response every time within a week of sending each mailing," he says. His steadily expanding client roster has allowed him to open a second office in his native Madrid, as well as to explore the possibilities of computerizing his entire portfolio presentation.

▲ *Javier Romero's prolific self-promotion (continued on following page) builds awareness through postcards, mailers, and ads in major talent directories. "I couldn't do without it," he says.*

▲ *Anything goes in Romero's self-promotion. His mailings are so effective that he gets responses within a week of mailing them*

▲ Romero's promotions are eye-catching, exciting and colorful.

## SIMPLE PLEASURES

*Gina Federico*
*Graphic Design*
*New Canaan, Connecticut*

Promotion for Gina Federico's graphic design studio stems from her own personal exuberance about life. "When something good or exciting happens," she says, "I like to let people know about it." Such a happy occasion can be a move to a new office, a change of studio affiliation, or simply the start of a new year. In any case, Federico's mailer-celebration is apt to be a simple execution, with a visual pun or other twist to make it memorable. Because she works alone, Federico strives to keep costs down, too, letting the concept, rather than its production, create the impression. "It's not marketing *per se*," she explains. "That's more or less a by-product." Still, Federico's low profile has earned her some plums—her work has been shown in the national design press and her business volume has grown steadily to where she's been able to establish her own independent design office.

▲ *Gina Federico's greeting cards are simple productions*

*that cost about two hundred dollars a year*

Change
of a
dress.

71 Park Place
New Canaan
Connecticut
06840

Gina Federico
graphic designer

203.966.7603

▲ *"Change of a dress" notice brought requests for samples of it from around the United States. Printing was done gratis*

## MADE FOR AMERICA

*Etienne Delessert*
*Lakeville, Connecticut*

Several years back, illustrator Etienne Delessert ran a large studio in Switzerland, where he and forty other artists produced books, films, and other large, collective works. But when he and his American wife, graphic designer Rita Marshall, decided to move to the United States, Delessert saw an opening for a radical career change: Tired of the big-studio pressure cooker, he retired to pastoral northern Connecticut, where he could reestablish a more personal relationship with his work. His first and only major promotion upon reaching these shores is still in use—a collection of illustrations, story boards, and ads collected into a twenty-four-page, full-color booklet. At a cost of four thousand dollars for three thousand copies, however, Delessert feels this was one project he overproduced. "I've only sent out two or three hundred copies," he says, "mostly to magazine art directors and friends, and already I have more work than I can handle." Having become established in the United States, his work how takes additional support from the occasional posters he and Marshall create to announce his speaking engagements. "My work speaks for itself," says Delessert. "Things tend to fall in place, so that I have a steady increase from year to year, both in work and in compensation."

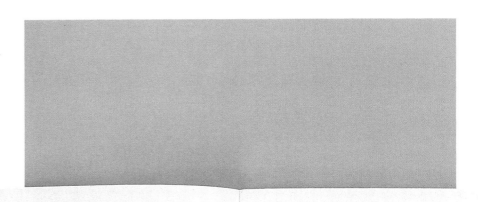

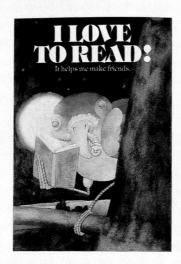

*Illustrator Etienne Delessert's twenty-four-page*

*sample booklet provides art directors with a real keeper*

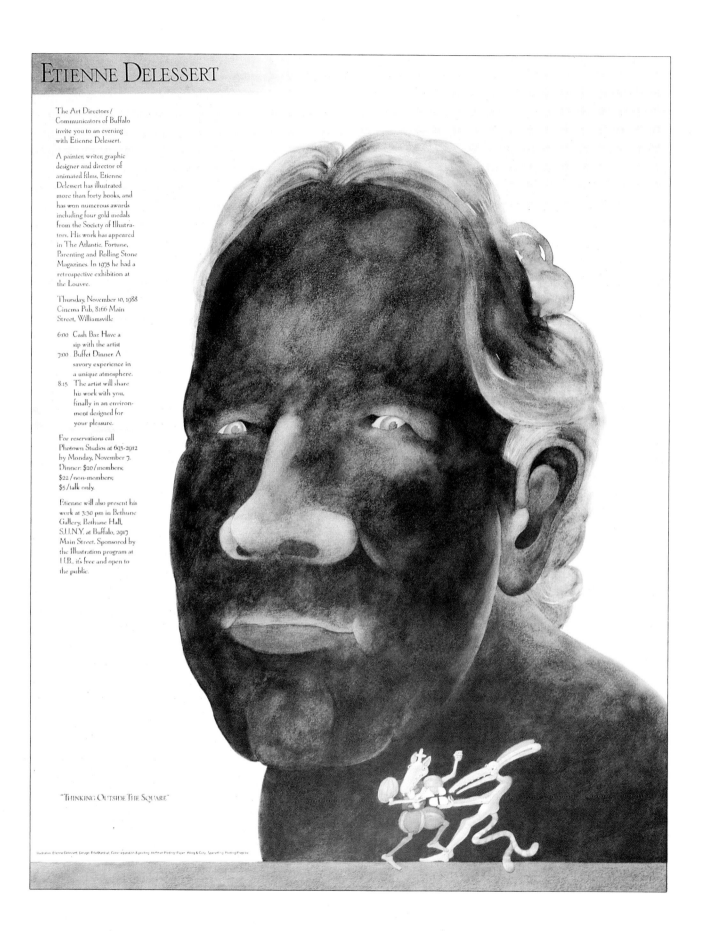

# ETIENNE DELESSERT

The Art Directors/
Communicators of Buffalo
invite you to an evening
with Etienne Delessert.

A painter, writer, graphic
designer and director of
animated films, Etienne
Delessert has illustrated
more than forty books, and
has won numerous awards
including four gold medals
from the Society of Illustrators. His work has appeared
in The Atlantic, Fortune,
Parenting and Rolling Stone
Magazines. In 1975 he had a
retrospective exhibition at
the Louvre.

Thursday, November 10, 1988
Cinema Pub, 8166 Main
Street, Williamsville

6:00  Cash Bar. Have a
      sip with the artist
7:00  Buffet Dinner. A
      savory experience in
      a unique atmosphere.
8:15  The artist will share
      his work with you,
      finally in an environ-
      ment designed for
      your pleasure.

For reservations call
Photown Studios at 693-2912
by Monday, November 7.
Dinner: $20/members;
$22/non-members;
$5/talk only.

Etienne will also present his
work at 3:30 pm in Bethune
Gallery, Bethune Hall,
S.U.N.Y. at Buffalo, 2917
Main Street. Sponsored by
the Illustration program at
U.B., it's free and open to
the public.

"THINKING OUTSIDE THE SQUARE"

*Self-portrait poster announcing Delessert's program with the Art Directors/Communicators of Buffalo (New York)*

## ANNUAL EFFORTS

*Fred Hartson*
*Graphic Design*
*Anaheim, California*

What began several years ago as a one-time, cooperative promotional effort has turned into an annual project for graphic designer Fred Hartson. By fortuitous circumstances, when photographer Gene Sasse approached Hartson with the idea of using some of his photographic images in a calendar, Hartson just happened to know a printer who in turn knew a color separator, who both wanted to promote their expanding businesses. That initial effort was so successful for all involved that, although players occasionally drop in or out, the game has continued ever since. And, because all services are donated, each of the participants saves a share of the estimated twenty-five thousand to thirty-five thousand dollars it would cost to print two hundred to fifteen hundred of each calendar. Too, it allows Hartson the chance to stretch his design sensibilities—as is especially apparent in his 1986 effort, which featured the Indian state of Ladakh. "These calendars are fun for me," Hartson says, "because I'm given free rein. And the printer's and engraver's sales reps are happy because they see the calendars hanging on agency walls all over town. They're a good reinforcement for initial sales presentations."

▲ *The "Extractions" calendar offers detailed views of everyday surfaces*

▲ Fred Hartson's 1986 "Ladakh" calendar has a handmade quality that builds on the rich yet simple textures of the East

## ANNUAL STRATEGISTS

*Frankfurt Gips Balkind
New York, New York, and
Hollywood, California*

In a series of four spread ads aimed at corporate communicators and marketing executives, communications designers Frankfurt Gips Balkind sought to break away from design-y soft sells and make a statement about the *business* of annual reports. "We're not like other design groups," says copy strategist Harriett Levin Balkind. "Our partners have diverse skills. Aubrey Balkind is an MBA; Steve Frankfurt is the former president of Young & Rubicam; Phil Gips is a great designer." This unique blend of talents is well expressed in the ad campaign, which devotes a spread to each of four FGB services—strategy, design, technology, and advertising. Produced in-house and placed for the cost of space in the annual report-oriented *AR*, the campaign brought in one sure annual report client and a number of inquiries. But more important, it served to set Frankfurt Gips Balkind apart as a design company dedicated to making business understandable.

▲ Frankfurt Gips Balkind's four-spread advertisement

*positions FGB as a design group dedicated to making business understandable*

## CORPORATE AND CAPABLE

*Jack Hough Associates
Norwalk, Connecticut, and
New York, New York*

The design capabilities book produced by graphic designers Jack Hough Associates reflects the clean, clear standards the firm sets for its corporate clients. Though it took the design firm ten years to produce the book, president Jack Hough feels strongly about the importance of such a lasting effort. "We were already a fairly well-known firm when we did this book," he says, "and we wanted to give substance to our name, to get into people's minds as well as their files." By reproducing strong imagery from client publications, the book quickly associates Jock Hough Associates with an impressive array of clients. "And people do hang on to these books," Hough adds. "We get calls from people who received them two or three years ago." Also kept in recipient files are the promotions the Hough office creates for major paper companies who supply the kinds of paper bought by Hough's clients. Here again, the challenge is to produce something that graphic designers and other paper specifiers will want to hang onto. Two such promotions, created by Hough's partner, Tom Morin, for Champion International, rely on somewhat spectacular coverage of unusual subject matter—the annual Iditarod sled-dog race in Alaska and the towns in the United States named Champion—for their holding power. Another—for Potlatch—provides corporate communications designers with a photographic clip-book.

▲ *Promotions created by Jack Hough Associates for Champion International focus on unusual subject matter. "The Last Great Race"—about the dogs and mushers of the Iditarod sled-dog race—is one of the client's most successful promotions ever.*

### Jack Hough Associates

### Stamford Center for the Arts

Capturing the spirit of an event and generating visual excitement are often critical elements in the success of a communications program.

The jazz of Ella Fitzgerald...the be-bop trumpet of Dizzy Gillespie...the expressive routines of the Pilobolus Dance Theatre ...these and other world-class performances served as the basis for a lively identity program Jack Hough Associates designed for the Stamford Center for the Arts — Connecticut's premier performing arts showcase.

The bright, four-color graphics, applied to a variety of communications, from advertising to theatre posters, T-shirts and tickets, provide the Center with an unmistakable and memorable identity and extend its vitality into the community at large.

Subscribe Now—
A Dazzling New
Season Will
Unfold Before
Your Eyes

▲ *Jack Hough Associates' capabilities brochure links the design firm with an impressive array of clients and projects*

# PERMISSIONS

## Page 4

Design firm: Paul Shaw/Letter
Design, New York City
Designer/calligrapher: Paul Shaw

## Page 6

Client/design firm: Pentagram Design,
London, New York City,
and San Francisco

## Page 10

Client/design firm: Wallace Church
Associates, New York City
Art directors: Stanley Church,
Bob Wallace
Designers: Stanley Church
Photographer: Louis Wallach
Copywriter: Robert Wallace, Jr.

## Page 12

Client: Champion International
Corporation
Designer: James Miho,
Pasadena, California
Photographer: James Miho
(Colorcast cover)
Copywriters: James Miho
(China, Colorcast cover);
Tony MacDowell
(Colorcast cover)

## Page 14

Client/design firm: Landor Associates,
San Francisco

## Page 16

Client/design firm: Carbone Smolan
Associates, New York City
Art directors: Kenneth Carbone,
Leslie Smolan
Designers: Eric A. Pike, Tom Walker
(Ten), Alison March
(Desserts)
Photographers: Irvin Blitz
(Desserts), various (Ten)

Copywriters: Rita D. Jacobs (Ten),
Susan Candell (Desserts)

## Page 17

Client: Paper Sources International
Design firm: Carbone Smolan
Associates, New York City
Art director: Kenneth Carbone
Designer: Claire Taylor
Copywriter: Mil Roseman

## Page 18

Client/design firm: Ken White +
Associates, Los Angeles
Art director: Ken White
Designers: Lisa Levin (White on White);
Bob Dinetz (Red-nosed
Christmas); Sylvia
Zimmerman, Lisa Pogue
(New office celebration)
Illustrator: Sylvia Zimmerman
(New office celebration)
Copywriter: Michelle Martino
(New office celebration)

## Page 20

Client/design firm: Belyea Design,
Seattle, Washington
Designer: Patricia Belyea

## Page 21

Client: Impression Northwest
Design firm: Belyea Design,
Seattle, Washington
Art director/designer: Patricia Belyea
Illustrators: Brian Holtzinger
(Bookmarks), Linda
Greenum (Bookplates)

## Page 22

Client/design firm: Michelle
Friesenhahn Design,
San Antonio, Texas
Art director/designer:
Michelle Friesenhahn
Photographers: Joe Chavanell,

Ric Kroninger, Reuben Njaa
Illustrators: Dan Soder, Val Stein, Bill
Washington, Michelle
Friesenhahn
Copywriters: Jeri Robison-Turner,
Michelle Friesenhahn

## Page 23

Client/design firm: Tracy Sabin
Illustration & Design,
San Diego, California
Designer/illustrator: Tracy Sabin

## Page 24

Client: Gordon Screen Printing
Design firm: Tracy Sabin
Illustration & Design,
San Diego, California
Designer/illustrator: Tracy Sabin

## Page 26

Client/design firm: Taylor &
Browning Design
Associates, Toronto,
Ontario
Art directors: Scott Taylor,
Paul Browning
Designers: Peter Baker and
John Sheng (Wine bottle)
Designer/illustrator: Peter Baker
(T-shirt)

## Page 28

Client/illustrator: Stephen Alcorn,
Cambridge, New York
Designer: John Alcorn

## Page 30

Client/design firm: Tharp Did It,
Los Gatos, California
Art director: Rick Tharp
Designers: Karen Nomura, Rick Tharp,
Kim Tomlinson, Jana Heer
Illustrators: Rick Tharp, Andrea Kelley
Photographers: Kelly O'Connor,
Franklin Avery
Copywriters: Ernie Brower, Charles

Drummond, Victor Cross,
James Smith, Rick Tharp

### Page 33

Client/design firm:  Weymouth
                Design, Inc., Boston
Art director:  Michael Weymouth
Designers:  Jose Lizardo (Brochure);
                Jose Lizardo, Tom Laidlaw
                (Ads)
Photographers:  Mike Weymouth,
                George Simian, Clint
                Clemens (Ads); various
                (Brochure)
Copywriter:  Michael Weymouth

### Page 34

Client/Illustrator: Andrea Eberbach
Design firm: Celeste Design
Art director/designer:
                Celeste Conover

### Page 36

Client/design firm: The Dunlavey
                Studio, Sacramento,
                California
Art director: Michael Dunlavey
Designers: Lindy Dunlavey (Tie, Stone,
                Paperweight), Sheree Lum
                Orsi   (Paperweight), Heidi
                Tomlinson (Brochure)
Photographers: Don Satterlee,
                Cathy Kelly (Brochure)
Fabricator: Jill Kuwamoto Oyung (Tie)
Copywriters: Michael and Lindy
                Dunlavey; Lynda Gianforte
                Mansfield (Brochure)

### Page 39

Clients: Curry Design, Skil-Set
                Typographers, B&S House
                of Printing, Graphic Magic
Design firm: Curry Design,
                Los Angeles
Art directors/designers: Steve Curry,
                Jason Scheideman
Photographers: Mark Scott

Illustrator: Steve Curry
Copywriters: Steve Curry,
                Jason Scheideman

### Page 41

Clients: Rick Eiber Design, Unicraft,
                Color Control (Brochure),
                The Type Gallery (Posters)
Design firm: Rick Eiber Design,
                Seattle, Washington
Art director: Rick Eiber
Designers: Rick Eiber (All);
                Rick Eiber, Tom Draper
                (Digital poster)

### Page 43

Client/designer: Renee Sullivan,
                Burlingame, California
Illustrator: Renee Sullivan

### Page 44

Client/design firm: Donovan and
                Green, New York City
Art directors: Michael Donovan,
                Nancye L. Green
Designers/copywriters: Michael
                Donovan, Nancye L. Green,
                Jenny Barry

### Page 45

Client/design firm: Frazier Design,
                San Francisco
Art director/copywriter:
                Craig Frazier
Designers: Craig Frazier,
                Deborah Hagemann,
                Grant Peterson

### Page 47

Client/design firm: Graffito,
                Baltimore, Maryland
Art director: Tim Thompson
Designers: Dave Plunkert, Joe
                Parisi (All)
Illustrators: Joe Parisi, Dave Plunkert

Photographer: Lightstruck Studios
Copywriters: Tony Mafale (Promo
                folder), Graffito (Others)

### Page 49

Client/design firm: Michael P.
                Cronan Design,
                San Francisco
Art director/designer/illustrator:
                Michael P. Cronan

### Page 50

Client/design firm: The Weller
                Institute for the Cure
                of Design, Park City, Utah
Art director/designer/copywriter:
                Don Weller

### Page 51

Client: Communication Artists
                of New Mexico
Design firm: The Weller Institute for
                the Cure of Design,
                Park City, Utah
Art director/designer/illustrator/
                copywriter: Don Weller

### Page 51

Client: Sinclair Printing
Design firm: The Weller Institute for
                the Cure of Design,
                Park City, Utah
Art director: Harold Burch
Designer/illustrator: Don Weller
Photographer: Michael Schoenfeld

### Page 52

Client: The Design Conference that
                Just Happens to Be in
                Park City
Design firm: The Weller Institute for
                the Cure of Design,
                Park City, Utah
Art director/designer/illustrator:
                Don Weller
Copywriters: Jon Anderson, Mikio
                Osaki, Don Weller

Copywriters: Peter Caroline, Doris
    Vemay (Copywriter ad)


## Page 94

Client/design firm: Chermayeff &
    Geismar Associates,
    New York City
Designers: Chermayeff &
    Geismar Associates


## Page 95

Client/design firm: Manhattan
    Design, New York City
Art directors: Frank Olinsky,
    Pat Gorman
Designer: Frank Olinsky
Photographer: Caroline Greyshock
Copywriters: Marty Pekar and
    Manhattan Design


## Page 96

Client/design firm: Concrete/The
    Office of Jilly Simons,
    Chicago, Illinois
Art director: Jilly Simons
Designers: Jilly Simons (All), David
    Robson (Concrete block),
    Joe VanDerBos
    (Concrete block, Holiday
    hiatus)
Fabricator: Franco Vecchio
    (Concrete block)


## Page 97

Client/design firm: Rod Dyer
    Group, Los Angeles
Art directors/designers: Rod Dyer
    (Restaurant, Design and
    advertising brochures),
    Henry Rosenthal (Motion
    picture and theater
    advertising brochures),
    Steve Twigger (Rooster
    moving campaign)
Illustrators: Henry Rosenthal (Motion
    picture and theater

advertising brochures),
    Paul Leith (Rooster moving
    campaign)


## Page 99

Client/design firm: Waters
    Design Associates,
    New York City
Art director: John Waters
Designers: John Waters, Dana
    Gonsalves (Business papers)
Illustrators/copywriters: John Waters,
    Margaret Riegel, Robert P.
    Kellerman, Dana Gonsalves,
    Ronald Leighton, Carol
    Bouyoucos
Photographers: David Arky


## Page 101

Client: James River Corporation
Design firm: Waters Design
    Associates,  New York City
Art director: John Waters
Designers/illustrators: Dana
    Gonsalves (Tuscan),
    Carol Bouyoucus
    (Curtis  Linen)
Copywriter: Peter Maloney


## Page 102

Client/design firm:
    Fitch RichardsonSmith,
    Worthington, Ohio
Art directors: Jaimie Alexander
    (Brochure); Michael
    Westcott (Christmas card);
    Kerry Bierman (Packaging
    postcards); Graham
    Freeman, Kate Murphy
    (Retail brochure)
Designers: Eric Weissinger, Robert
    Thomas (Brochure); Kun-Tee
    Chang (Christmas card);
    Paul Westrick, Kwok C.
    Chan (Packaging
    postcards); Roderick
    Johnson (Retail brochure)

Photographers: Various
Illustrator: Kate Hanlon
    (Christmas card)
Copywriters: Michael Floreak
    (Brochure, Christmas card);
    Mike Mooney (Packaging
    postcards); Graham
    Freeman, Kate Murphy
    (Retail brochure)


## Page 104

Client/design firm: Anthony
    Russell, Inc.,
    New York City
Art director: Anthony Russell
Designers: Anthony Russell, Sam Kuo,
    Casey Clark
Photographers/illustrators: Various
Copywriters: Anthony Russell
    (Quarterlies, Fishing
    promo);  Michael
    O'Connor (U.S. Eye)


## Page 106

Client/design firm: Mike Quon
    Design Office,
    New York City
Art director/designer: Mike Quon
Photographer/illustrator: Mike Quon


## Page 108

Client: Warren's Waller Press
Design firm: The Office of
    Michael  Manwaring,
    San Francisco
Designer: Michael Manwaring
Copywriter: Maureen Oddone


## Page 109

Client: Mitsumura Printing
Design firm: Gerald Reis & Com-
pany,            San Francisco
Designer/illustrator: Gerald Reis

**Page 111**

Client/illustrator: Alan E. Cober, Ossining, New York
Art director: John de Cesare (Corporate cober)
Designers: Kent Dicken (Corporate Cober mailer), Dan Kovasckitz (Wake-up call), Kurt Gibson (Dollar bills)
Copywriters: Kent Dicken, Alan Cober, John de Cesare (Corporate cober), Jack Dillard (Wake-up call), Steven Heller (Dollar bills)

**Page 113**

Client/design firm: Summerford Design, Dallas, Texas
Art director/designer: Jack Summerford
Photographer: John Katz
Copywriter: Jack Summerford

**Page 115**

Client/design firm: R.L. Meyer Advertising, Milwaukee, Wisconsin
Designer/copywriter: R.L. Meyer Advertising

**Page 118**

Client/designer/illustrator: Steven Guarnaccia, New York City

**Page 120**

Client/design firm: Samata Associates, Dundee, Illinois
Art directors/designers: Pat and Greg Samata
Photographers: Jean Moss (Memories), Mark Joseph (Recipes)
Illustrators: George Sawa (Memories),

Paul Thompson (Recipes, Masks)
Copywriters: Nancy Bishop/Samata Associates (Recipes, Memories), Steve Huggins (Masks)
Mask Designer: Brenda Lee Tracy

**Page 121**

Client/design firm: The Ink Tank, New York City
Art director/designer: R.O. Blechman
Illustrators: R.O. Blechman (All); Gary Baseman, Isabelle Dervaux (Ad, Mailer); Santiago Cohen, Laszlo Kubinyi (Mailer); Maciek Albrecht (Ad)

**Page 123**

Client/design firm: Koppel & Scher, New York City
Art director/designers/copywriters: Terry Koppel, Paula Scher

**Page 125**

Client: Champion International
Design firm: Koppel & Scher, New York City
Designer/illustrator: Paula Scher

**Page 126**

Client: Weyerhauser Paper Company
Ad agency: Fallon McElligott, Minneapolis, Minnesota
Design firm: McCool & Company, Minneapolis, Minnesota
Art director: Dean Hanson/ Fallon McElligott (Inserts)
Designers: Todd Nesser and Jo Davison Strand/McCool & Company (Collateral)
Photographer: Dan Peace
Copywriters: Phil Hanft/Fallon McElligott (Inserts), Corinne Mitchell/McCool & Company (Collateral)

**Page 128**

Client/design firm: Hornall Anderson Design Works, Seattle, Washington
Art directors: Jack Anderson, John Hornall
Designers: Jack Anderson, John Hornall (All); David McDougall (Binder, T-shirt); Cliff Chung (Lobby sign); Julie Tanagi-Lock (Invitation); Brian O'Neill (Stationery)
Copywriter: John Hornall (Invitation)

**Page 129**

Client: Print Northwest
Design firm: Hornall Anderson Design Works, Seattle, Washington
Art director: Jack Anderson
Designers: Jack Anderson, Heidi Hatlestad (Identity program, Brochure); Jani Drewfs (Brochure)
Photographer: Edmund Lowe (Brochure)
Illustrators: Scott McDougall (Identity program, Brochure); Tim Kilian, Rod Ambroson, Georgia Peaver, Cheri Ryan (Brochure)
Copywriter: Fran Olsen (Brochure)

**Page 130**

Client: Neenah Paper
Design firm: Hornall Anderson Design Works, Seattle, Washington
Art directors: Jack Anderson, Juliet Shen
Designers: Juliet Shen, John Hornall
Photographers/illustrators: Various
Copywriter: Margy Tylczak, Dory Toft

# Other Art Books from North Light

## Graphics/Business of Art

**Airbrush Artist's Library (6 in series)** $12.95 (cloth)
**Airbrush Techniques Workbooks (8 in series)** $9.95 each
**Airbrushing the Human Form**, by Andy Charlesworth $27.95 (cloth)
**The Art & Craft of Greeting Cards**, by Susan Evarts $15.95 (paper)
**The Artist's Friendly Legal Guide**, by Conner, Karlen, Perwin, & Spatt $15.95 (paper)
**Artist's Market: Where & How to Sell Your Graphic Art (Annual Directory)** $18.95 (cloth)
**Basic Graphic Design & Paste-Up**, by Jack Warren $13.95 (paper)
**Color Harmony: A Guide to Creative Color Combinations**, by Hideaki Chijiiwa $15.95 (paper)
**Complete Airbrush & Photoretouching Manual**, by Peter Owen & John Sutcliffe $23.95 (cloth)
**The Complete Guide to Greeting Card Design & Illustration**, by Eva Szela $27.95 (cloth)
**Creating Dynamic Roughs**, by Alan Swann $27.95 (cloth)
**Creative Ad Design & Illustration**, by Dick Ward $32.95 (cloth)
**Creative Director's Sourcebook**, by Nick Souter and Stuart Neuman $89.00 (cloth)
**Creative Typography**, by Marion March $27.95 (cloth)
**Design Rendering Techniques**, by Dick Powell $29.95 (cloth)
**Dynamic Airbrush**, by David Miller & James Effler $29.95 (cloth)
**Fashion Illustration Workbooks (4 in series)** $8.95 each
**Fantasy Art**, by Bruce Robertson $24.95 (cloth)
**Getting It Printed**, by Beach, Shepro & Russon $29.50 (paper)
**The Graphic Artist's Guide to Marketing & Self-Promotion**, by Sally Prince Davis $15.95 (paper)
**The Graphic Arts Studio Manual**, by Bert Braham $22.95 (cloth)
**Graphic Tools & Techniques**, by Laing & Saunders-Davies $24.95 (cloth)
**Graphics Handbook**, by Howard Munce $14.95 (paper)
**Handbook of Pricing & Ethical Guidelines**, 6th edition, by The Graphic Artist's Guild $19.95 (paper)
**How to Design Trademarks & Logos**, by Murphy & Row $24.95 (cloth)
**How to Draw & Sell Cartoons**, by Ross Thomson & Bill Hewison $17.95 (cloth)
**How to Draw & Sell Comic Strips**, by Alan McKenzie $18.95 (cloth)
**How to Draw Charts & Diagrams**, by Bruce Robertson $24.95 (cloth)
**How to Understand & Use Design & Layout**, by Alan Swann $24.95 (cloth)
**How to Understand & Use Grids**, by Alan Swann $27.95 (cloth)
**How to Write and Illustrate Children's Books**, edited by Treld Pelkey Bicknell and Felicity Trotman, $22.50 (cloth)
**Illustration & Drawing: Styles & Techniques**, by Terry Presnall $22.95 (cloth)
**Living by Your Brush Alone**, by Edna Wagner Piersol $16.95 (paper)
**Marker Rendering Techniques**, by Dick Powell & Patricia Monahan $32.95 (cloth)
**Marker Techniques Workbooks (8 in series)** $9.95 each
**The North Light Art Competition Handbook**, by John M. Angelini $9.95 (paper)
**North Light Dictionary of Art Terms**, by Margy Lee Elspass $10.95 (paper)
**Papers for Printing**, by Mark Beach & Ken Russon $34.50 (paper)
**Preparing Your Design for Print**, by Lynn John $27.95 (cloth)
**Presentation Techniques for the Graphic Artist**, by Jenny Mulherin $24.95 (cloth)
**Print Production Handbook**, by David Bann $14.95 (cloth)
**Ready to Use Layouts for Desktop Design**, by Chris Prior $27.95 (cloth)
**Studio Secrets for the Graphic Artist**, by Jack Buchan $29.95 (cloth)
**Type: Design, Color, Character & Use**, by Michael Beaumont $24.95 (cloth)
**Using Type Right**, by Philip Brady $18.95 (paper)

**To order directly from the publisher, include $3.00 postage and handling for one book, 50¢ for each additional book. Allow 30 days for delivery.**

**North Light Books**
**1507 Dana Avenue, Cincinnati, Ohio 45207**
Credit card orders
Call TOLL-FREE
1-800-289-0963
Prices subject to change without notice.